Unspeakable
Losses

W. W. Norton & Company

New York • London

Unspeakable Losses

UNDERSTANDING
THE EXPERIENCE OF
PREGNANCY LOSS, MISCARRIAGE,
AND ABORTION

Kim Kluger-Bell

For information about permission to reproduce selections from this book, write to Permissions, W. W. Norton & Company, Inc., 500 Fifth Avenue, New York, NY 10110.

The text of this book is composed in Bembo with the display set in Lichten.
Composition by White River Publishing Services
Manufacturing by Quebecor Printing Book Group
Book design by Judith Stagnitto Abbate

Library of Congress Cataloging-in-Publication Data

Kluger-Bell, Kim.
    Unspeakable losses : understanding the experience of pregnancy loss, miscarriage, and abortion / Kim Kluger-Bell.
        p.   cm.
    Includes bibliographical references.
    ISBN 0-393-04572-2
    1. Miscarriage—Psychological aspects. 2. Stillbirth—Psychological aspects. 3. Abortion—Psychological aspects. 4. Bereavement—Psychological aspects. I. Title.
RG648.K56 1998
618.3'92'019—dc21   97-13398

W. W. Norton & Company, Inc., 500 Fifth Avenue, New York, N.Y. 10110
http://www.wwnorton.com

W. W. Norton & Company Ltd., 10 Coptic Street, London, WC1A 1PU

1 2 3 4 5 6 7 8 9 0

For Barry and Max,
who never lost their faith
during this arduous journey together;
and
For the daughter I wished for:
it was her absence that brought this book
into being.

Contents

Acknowledgments

First and foremost, I would like to thank the people I interviewed and the patients I have worked with, for their generosity in speaking with me, answering my many questions, and giving me permission to tell their stories. Their stories make up the backbone of this book, and their willingness to speak openly about their experiences will encourage many others to give voice to their own silent grief.

I am also deeply grateful to those who freely gave of their time and expertise during the book's "gestation." This includes—but is not limited to—Carla Harkness, who first encouraged me to pursue this project when it was barely a gleam in my eye; my dear friend Peggy O'Neil, M.F.C.C., who, despite reading endless versions of this manuscript, never lost her enthusiasm for the book; my "cheerleader" Judith Watkins, M.F.C.C.; my very helpful editor Lucy Anderson; and my colleagues Kathy Anolick, M.F.C.C., Betty Cohn Simpson, L.C.S.W., Jean Benward, L.C.S.W., Yvonne Rand, Dr. Jeanne Menary, and Dr. Sue Elkind, all of whose professional expertise was instrumental in shaping the direction of this work, and enriching it immensely. Special thanks also to Jane Lewenthal and Susan Willman, M.D., for their networking assistance.

For meticulously transcribing many interviews and offering invaluable insights I would like to thank my good friend Linda

Witnov. For indispensable research assistance, editorial help and enthusiasm, I thank Amanda Johnsen. For reliable encouragement I would like to thank my sister and fellow author, Lili Bell Shelton and my writing partner, Lucy Hilmer.

And for their steadfast faith in the merits of this project, and in my own abilities as a writer, I would like to express my heartfelt gratitude to Jeri Marlowe and my husband, Barry Kluger-Bell; as well as my beloved editor, Jill Bialosky, and my agent, Beth Vesel, who so ably assisted in the birth of this book.

Preface

A NUMBER OF years ago, in a daze following my second pregnancy loss, I found myself combing the shelves of a well-stocked local bookstore, trying to find something that would assure me that the relentless despair I was experiencing was anywhere close to being normal. No one around me seemed able to provide that reassurance, and I was beginning to feel there was something seriously wrong with me for being so preoccupied by an event that I should have been able to put behind me many weeks before.

Even my training as a psychotherapist did little to soothe me. I could find no professional resource book on the psychological impact of pregnancy loss, and even the *Diagnostic and Statistical Manual of Mental Disorders*—the authoritative reference for mental health professionals—did not include pregnancy loss among the significant life stressors which could be expected to result in the kind of distress I was experiencing. This led me to the uneasy conclusion that my obsession with this relatively minor loss was clearly pathological.

My family and friends were concerned about me, but most were silent on the subject of my pregnancy loss. No one seemed to know what to say. I was beginning to feel that my enduring anguish was a source of discomfort for everyone around me and yet no one, it seemed, knew how to help.

The many shelves of books on pregnancy, childbirth and childrearing did not contain a single volume on the topic of pregnancy loss. When I finally found the courage to inquire at the front counter, I was directed to a dark corner in the back of the bookstore where a single shelf contained several books on infertility and one on pregnancy loss which I had already purchased some time before.

I left the bookstore feeling humiliated. A few months before I had browsed happily through the impressive array of books on pregnancy and left contentedly with an armload of books. Now, having lost the baby I was carrying, I felt abruptly excluded from that world of happy anticipation and thrust rudely into its other, darker side, a shadow side where there were no friendly guides to show the way. When I got through this, I told myself, I would write one of the books I had been looking for that day.

This is that book. I spent nearly a year interviewing people who had experienced pregnancy losses of all kinds—from ectopic pregnancies and failed in vitro fertilization attempts to miscarriages, stillbirths and abortions. I spoke with numerous doctors, counselors, and therapists who treat patients affected by these reproductive crises. I uncovered all the existing literature I could on the topic, and paid close attention to the process of recovering from these traumas by drawing both on my own experience and the experience of my psychotherapy patients.

I hope this book will serve as a companion for anyone who has ever suddenly fallen through to the other side of pregnancy—by means of pregnancy loss, abortion or infertility—and has felt the need for a knowledgeable guide. I also hope it will assist friends, family members, nurses, doctors and psychotherapists in learning how to accompany someone on this difficult journey.

This may not be an easy book to read. It is uncomfortable to witness the suffering of others: it makes us aware of how powerless we are to control so many aspects of our lives, or to help others manage theirs. There is always the impulse to turn away from what might disturb us. But the reader who perseveres will find the stories in these pages to be tales of struggle, courage, and ultimately of transformation, all attesting to the remarkable vitality of the human spirit.

> . . . the little grasses
> Crack through stone, and they are green with life.[1]
> — S Y L V I A   P L A T H

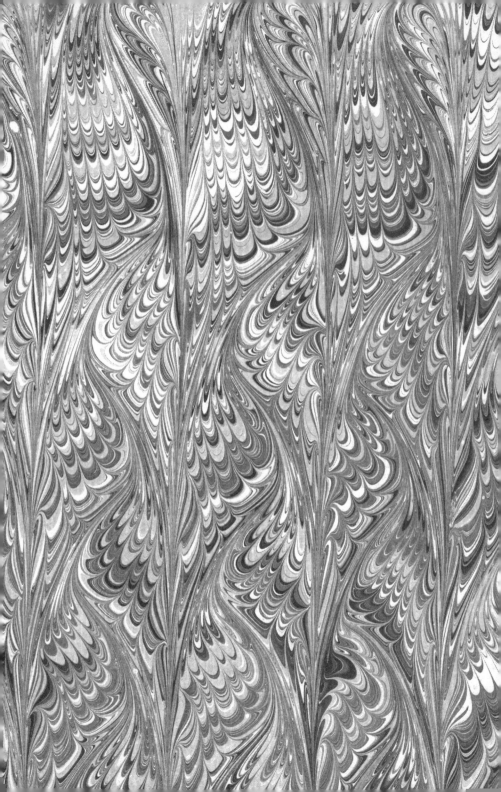

ONE

Silent Suffering

I HAVE A *dreamlike image of waiting, terrified, outside my mother's bathroom door knowing only that she is sitting on the toilet and bleeding. I think she is calling to me to get her some sanitary napkins and I can't find them and she is panicky and I don't know what is happening.*

I must have been about ten years old at the time. My mother ended up in the hospital. My father told me later that she'd had a miscarriage. I'd never heard the word before but the way he said it made me think that I shouldn't ask too many questions. He told me, though, that it meant she had been pregnant and that she had lost the baby. I think he said it had been a boy and that I shouldn't tell anyone else, even my younger sisters, because they were too little and they wouldn't understand.

I remember being astounded that I might have had a little brother—that he was there and now he was gone. But not another word was ever spoken about the incident and my memory of it receded into that hazy half-known place where things might just as well be dreams as actual events.

Many years later, a married college friend of mine had a miscarriage. I remember going to visit her not long after it happened and being surprised by how upset she was. Her tears were incomprehensible to me. I had spent most of my adult life being convinced that I could become pregnant in a heartbeat, and I was trying conscientiously to avoid that dreaded state. Though I muttered some sympathetic words to her, secretly I condemned her for her exaggerated reaction. My god, she was behaving as though someone close to her had died!

Fifteen years after my friend had her miscarriage I was sitting in a class, having recently found out that I was pregnant with my second, badly wanted child. Suddenly, I felt a rush of warm blood come gushing out of me. With it came the long-buried terror surrounding my mother's miscarriage, but I was convinced that if I could hold on tightly enough I could save the baby we had been trying more than two years to conceive.

Every few hours I had been checking myself for signs of blood: whether it was brown or red, how much there was of it. My doctor had been monitoring my hormone levels with sensitive blood tests every few days too. If the numbers didn't go up quickly enough I was in for either a miscarriage or an ectopic pregnancy. Nothing was definitive until I saw the blood: bright red and flowing freely. I tried to stop it up with toilet paper. I tried to sit very, very still. I tried to cross my legs and hold it in. But still it came. I could feel it flowing out of me, my lifeblood, my baby.

On the way to the hospital I felt as though I were observing this scene from a distance, as if it were happening to someone else, a long time ago.

These are the echoes of ancient losses, pebbles tossed carelessly into the pond, reverberating with past and future significance. There is hardly a life untouched by a pregnancy loss, and yet each one seems so unknowable and unknown. We seem to have no words to name our experiences of these losses. Or perhaps we turn away in an attempt to avoid a confrontation with one of life's darkest and cruelest twists, a life ended before it begins.

These are the facts: Every year 890,000 of the 6.5 million pregnancies in the United States end in some form of miscarriage or stillbirth and another 1.5 million end in abortion.[1] In the space of one short year almost 2.5 million people are affected by pregnancy losses of one kind or another.

It is hard to imagine a statistic related to life and death that is more prevalent, yet at the same time less widely known. A woman in her early forties who had three miscarriages in a little over two years puts it this way:

> *I had never really realized how many miscarriages there were until I had one. That's when people would "come out" about it, and talk about their own miscarriages. Like they were coming out of the closet! But when it happened the first time I was really unprepared . . . it made me feel like there was something really wrong with me because I had never heard of anybody having them.*

How is it that we have not heard? That we do not know? Another woman describes her lack of preparation for the emotional impact of her abortion:

> *I wasn't prepared for the crisis I went through when I got pregnant accidentally after my fourth child. I grew up in the sixties. I had always thought about abortions as being a pretty straightforward medical procedure. I was—and still am—strongly in favor of a parent's right to choose whether to bear a child. But I wasn't at all prepared for my reaction when I was faced with that choice. I knew that for a lot of reasons we couldn't have another child but I couldn't bring myself to make that appointment. I postponed it for a really long time, until it was almost too late. I did finally go through with*

it and I know it was the right decision. But I felt ripped apart by the whole experience and on top of that I felt like I didn't have a right to feel so much grief and pain.

So I put it all out of my mind and I didn't tell anyone about it. My husband and I were the only ones who knew, and we didn't talk about it either.

A heavy shroud of silence surrounds pregnancy losses of any kind. These are private, intensely personal affairs. There is often shame and a desire to forget, and, especially with the chosen loss of abortion, a fear of condemnation, of being blamed for a deep parental failure.

Women sit in quiet rooms with friends who are recovering from recent losses and say, "Yes, I know how you feel. I had a miscarriage or a stillbirth or an abortion. I had one too." But rarely do they elaborate. It seems so hard to talk about. There is a hesitancy to say it out loud, to name the experience, to own it.

Perhaps part of the reason is that the losses of pregnancy seem so intangible and unreal, especially in the case of pregnancies which end before a heartbeat is heard, or an abdomen begins to swell. But even in the case of later pregnancy losses such as second-trimester miscarriages or stillbirths, there are no memories to hold on to, no life to recall outside of the womb, only fantasies of who these babies might have been.

It is also risky, in the current sociopolitical climate with regard to abortion, to talk about one's feelings following an abortion without fear of condemnation from either side of the debate. Women who admit to feelings of relief following abortions are condemned as heartless killers by the far religious right, while those who talk about feelings of loss and regret following abortions often feel like traitors to the pro-choice movement. Some women probably fear that if they speak too loudly of their grief following early miscarriages they will give fuel to the anti-abortion movement. Given this cultural climate, it is hardly surprising that those who have abortions and other forms of pregnancy loss rarely speak out about their experiences.

And for men, the silence is often even more profound. Not only is little or no encouragement given to men to openly mourn their own childbearing losses, but they are often condemned if they do so. A man whose wife had recently suffered a stillbirth describes his employer's reactions to his loss:

> *They gave me two days bereavement leave after our baby died. But my wife was feeling so bad that she didn't want to be alone and I knew I couldn't concentrate at work anyway so I took the whole week off. But when I called them they told me not to bother coming back at all. I guess they figured I was faking it, taking advantage of the situation. I know they thought they were being generous to give me two days off to grieve.*

Another man, whose girlfriend had opted for an abortion against his wishes ten years before, describes the anguish he felt he was not entitled to and therefore disowned. Men are rarely expected to be as emotionally engaged as women in the pregnancies they help to create, or to be just as affected by their loss:

> *At the time [of the abortion] I was almost completely focused on her. I really regret not having had the baby, even though our relationship was rocky and I knew she didn't feel confident enough about us being together to have the baby. She was really upset by the whole thing—having to make the decision to abort. I think I was more concerned about her feelings than anything else. Afterwards I felt relieved, because she was so much calmer, but I just felt numb and depressed. We never really talked about it afterwards.*

And perhaps the most invisible childbearing loss of all is the hidden grief of those who, after long delays in childbearing because of the lack of a suitable relationship or sufficient financial security, have been unable to have the children they wanted and always thought they would have. A woman in her early forties who had not yet found the stable relationship she yearned for describes her situation:

> *The baby years are gone and I'm really feeling the loss of them. But I don't get much sympathy from anyone at all. The few women friends I've talked to about it say I should just go out and try to have a child anyway, use a sperm bank or whatever. They really don't get it that that's not a solution for this pain.*

As a culture, we seem to have an intolerance for suffering; we tend to want those who have experienced a loss of any kind to get on with their lives as quickly as possible. Often, by minimizing the impact of significant losses, pathologizing those whose reactions are intense, and applauding those who seem relatively unaffected by tragic events, we encourage the inhibition of our grief. In both obvious and subtle ways, we tell those who grieve that they are wrong to be so upset, to dwell on their miseries.

A woman whose miscarriage was quickly followed by another, successful pregnancy describes the pressure she felt to forget about her loss:

> *Everyone told me to put the past behind me and get on with my life and keep trying for another baby. They told me it was meant to be and that it would probably never happen again. My friends were very sympathetic for the first week or so after the miscarriage but after that they stopped asking how I was doing. I assumed that meant they thought I should be doing just fine. When I turned down an invitation to a baby shower two months after my miscarriage one of my friends told me I shouldn't isolate myself so much.*
>
> *When I got pregnant again everyone thought I was completely over my miscarriage. When I told my sister that I was going to plant a tree on the due date of the baby I had lost she said she didn't think*

that was a good idea because it might create bad feelings for the baby
I was carrying.

Ours is such a youth-oriented and insistently optimistic culture.
For the most part, we refuse to acknowledge the inevitability of
death, the necessity of loss. Illness and aging are often viewed as
defects or personal failures: if only we had done the right things
we wouldn't have fallen prey to illness; if only there had been
enough research a cure would surely have been found. We seem to
believe that given enough effort and will power we can conquer
anything. Wanting to believe this as fervently as we do makes us
tend to turn away from the sick, the dying and the grieving. We
get angry with them and wish they would go away because they
are reminders, constant reminders, of the limitations of our power,
of the inevitability of our own demise.

Perhaps the utter powerlessness implied by the loss of an
unlived life is simply unacceptable. It may be too great a reminder
that despite all the modern-day medical miracles that have both
extended the human life span beyond what was thinkable even a
few generations ago and virtually assured the survival of even the
tiniest premature baby—despite all the control over life that we
have gained—death is our common destiny. Perhaps this is the
ultimate fact that we seek to avoid by our silence.

Unfortunately, though, if we cannot speak of our experiences
or even put them into words, we cannot know them. They are
banished to the underground of the unconscious where they can
continue to influence us without our knowing it. As Yvonne
Rand, a Soto Zen Buddhist priest who has spent many years helping those who have lost babies in pregnancy to come to terms
with their experiences, puts it: "If you cannot name your experience you cannot have any real closure, and you end up with an
emotional, psychological, spiritual dangling. People carry enormous, unrecognized grief for decades."

We carry our suffering in our bodies in excess body weight and chronic physical pain. Grief that is too painful to face is likely to become displaced into chronic depression or psychosomatic disorders. This frozen grief can be heard in our voices, in our cynical outlook on life, in our expectations of failure, in our longings for something undefinable, in our inability to empathize with the losses of others.

British psychologist John Bowlby, in his landmark study on the nature of attachment and loss, maintains that the goal of mourning is to accept the reality of the loved one's death and that most cultural traditions surrounding death are designed to assist mourners in dealing with their confusion about what has happened, "through bringing home the fact that a loss has in fact occurred."[2] Funerals and other ritual gatherings also tend to provide mourners an opportunity to publicly express their grief as well as help in defining the period through which mourning is appropriate. In the absence of such supports—combined with the absence of a visible baby to touch or to hold—would-be parents are faced with a "non-event, an unreality and no one to mourn."[3]

But working through grief involves learning to withstand the certainty and the finality of the loss, uncovering the personal significance of what has been lost, and neither holding on to nor pushing away the sorrow, anger, guilt, shame, despair and envy that arise in response to it. Obviously it is not possible to do this if most or all of the relevant thoughts and feelings are immediately repressed, denied or minimized—if the loss is never identified as being real.

When I failed to comprehend my college friend's despair following the miscarriage of her baby, I was responding to the silence following my mother's miscarriage and the subsequent repression of my emotional reactions to it. As a consequence, I was stunned by my own pregnancy loss and felt detached and unable to integrate the experience. And when after a second pregnancy loss I fought hard to keep the feelings of sadness, guilt, anger and despair from conscious awareness, I was following the script that my culture had written for me. A script which, unfortunately, didn't allow for the resolution of any of these experiences and left me isolated, ashamed and immobilized. More than three years after my first pregnancy loss and a year and a half after my final one, I made the following journal entry:

> *There is a hard knot of grief nestled under my right shoulder blade. It's about the size of a small fist and it's making it hard for me to move, hard to forget about my baby girl who should have been born—I realize now—a year ago today. Will I ever be over this?*

Sometimes this undigested sorrow remains buried until, many years later, it is triggered by an experience that has a fundamental similarity to the circumstances of the original loss. Twenty years after she had a miscarriage, a woman whose grown daughter had recently decided on an abortion describes the flood of grief and guilt and regret that swept over her.

> *I felt like crying. The loss of this—my first grandchild—seemed impossible to bear. I was furious with my daughter at first, but my heart went out to her when I could see how much she was struggling with this decision, how impossible it was for her to feel good about it either way. Eventually I started to understand that it was just as much the loss of my own first baby that I was feeling. Until that day, if anyone had asked me I would have said I was completely over the miscarriage. But actually, I took that miscarried baby and buried it before I had a chance to see it or understand what I'd lost.*

Grief, when allowed to progress naturally, tends to come in waves. After the first initial shock of the loss abates, waves of sorrow begin to wash over you rather unpredictably. At first the waves are huge and close together and you are afraid that you will drown. Eventually, they get smaller and more manageable, and you grow less afraid of them, although a big one can still take you by surprise. The phrase "working through" grief means that you are able to get to the point where you can just stand there and let the waves sweep over you and not try to run or pretend you're not getting soaked. Standing there feeling the waves, you start to realize that this is as bad as it's going to get and you begin to understand that you are going to survive. That's when you start to pass through to the other side of mourning: accepting and making peace with your loss.

The majority of people I have spoken to in my work as a psychotherapist, and those whom I interviewed for this book, have struggled to come to terms with their pregnancy losses. Getting to the point of simply being able to withstand the feelings these losses arouse often is no simple matter.

In the six years following the birth of my son I lost two ectopic pregnancies, requiring the removal of both fallopian tubes, and I also experienced four IVF (in vitro fertilization) failures in which living embryos were transferred to my womb but failed to implant. Like many others, I tried to distract myself from my sadness and pretend it wasn't there. My focus during those six long years was almost continually on trying to have another baby, and not on the babies I had lost. When the inevitable feelings of hopelessness, anger and envy arose, I condemned myself for being overly dramatic.

It is a fairly typical strategy for coping with these losses to keep the door shut tightly against one's sorrow. And as a result, the grieving process is often long and hard and slow. The tears I rejected came only when I slept. For six years I woke myself sobbing for those babies only in my dreams.

It was only when I began to give voice to my experiences, to speak of them first in journal writing and then out loud, that I was able to identify what I felt and what it meant to me. Hearing others say what they experienced helped to bring me out of the isolation and sense of shame that our culture's silence promotes. I found that, over time, the more I could allow my feelings in response to these losses to exist—the more I could leave the door open to my grief in whatever form it took—the more I could participate fully in my life again, and the more completely I could cherish it.

In what follows in this book, the silence surrounding pregnancy losses and abortions will be broken by many voices. Listening to them may benefit us all.

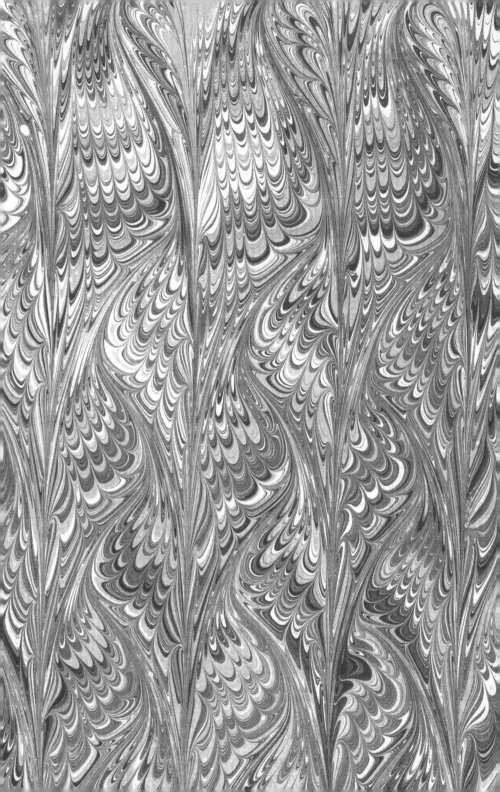

The Broken Promise: Early Losses

When a woman first realizes she is carrying a new life within her womb, her joy and sense of fulfillment may be mingled with wonder, but the pregnancy itself seems quite natural to her. . . . It is as though something within her said "This is the way it is to be a woman."

— M. ESTHER HARDING[1]

The essence of motherhood is a colossal swallowing up . . . a bursting of the ego.

— MARGUERITE DURAS[2]

HE DISCOVERY of a pregnancy—and the promise of a new life—is a moment of overwhelming intensity. Shock, excitement, anxiety and fear rush in. Each pregnancy has a unique meaning for each woman. This meaning is dictated not only by her life circumstances at the time of the discovery of the pregnancy—the nature of her relationship to her partner, whether the pregnancy was planned or unplanned, her age, her work commitments and her financial security—but also by her fundamental attitudes toward sexuality, pregnancy, childbearing, and motherhood, as well as her own earliest experiences of *being* mothered.

The beginning of a life embodies the promise of personal fulfillment and healing, a potential expansion of the self into the future and the hope for a reparation of childhood injuries. As Dr. Jeanne Menary, a psychologist who specializes in the psychological impact of genetic abortions, puts it: "A baby holds out a promise for the future . . . the promise for more life—feelings of greater wholeness, meaning, connection, and balance."[3] For many, a baby is hope incarnate.

By the same token, the seed of a new life can arouse primitive fears of abandonment and self-annihilation, a fear of the inevitable repetition of an unpleasant past. The range of experience is enormous.

One woman describes her experiences in pregnancy this way:

I have never felt so special, so singled out for attention as when I was pregnant. I felt I was capable of anything.

While another woman writes of hers:

The whole supposedly blessed experience of pregnancy is highly overrated. I was sick and bloated for nine months and I never felt I was "glowing." I felt intruded on.

Ambivalence—intense anxiety along with exhilaration—is characteristic of the early months of pregnancy. But so is a sense of unreality, when there are few visible signs of this momentous internal change. Consequently, the first gestational trimester (the first twelve weeks of the pregnancy, beginning with the first day of the last menstrual cycle) requires a dramatic adjustment to the reality of the beginning of a new life and a corresponding assumption of parental responsibilities in relation to it.

This process of adaptation often goes on without the knowledge of the world surrounding the pregnant woman and sometimes even without the knowledge of those closest to her. This growing accommodation to a new parental role is mirrored by the woman's swelling abdomen. And typically, the growing reality of the baby's existence is accompanied by an increasing emotional attachment.

Each day the pregnancy is one day closer to the reality of bringing home a baby. And so the images get conjured up and become stronger and more embedded into my head, so on day one all I ever imagined is a cute little baby, and by day two I know what he looks like and by day three I've got him enrolled somewhere in school and by day four I've got the christening in my mind and by day five we're having conversations and I know things I'm going to say to him . . . each day it gets more and more real.[4]

Until recently, this attachment was thought to have typically taken place at the moment of "quickening"—when the mother-to-be is first aware of the baby moving within her. This usually takes place between the twelfth and the fifteenth week of pregnancy, in the second trimester, and is often the time when the mother first becomes acutely aware of the existence of another being, separate from but intimately related to herself.

But these days, early blood tests that measure minute amounts of the pregnancy hormone HCG (human chorionic gonadotropin) can be used to confirm a pregnancy as early as five days after conception, while ultrasound monitoring often can be used to obtain a visual image of a fetus as early as six weeks after conception, and an instrument called a Doppler (or Doptone) can detect and amplify a fetal heartbeat as early as eleven weeks into the pregnancy. In many cases, not only do parents hear their baby's heartbeat before the end of the first trimester, but they know about the pregnancy before a menstrual period has been missed and they are able to view, along with the doctor or technician, an image of their embryonic offspring on a black-and-white television monitor. Sometimes they can even take home a photograph of it.

For the first time in human history, we have a window on the womb. And the more mechanisms we have developed to detect and visualize early fetal life, the sooner that life becomes real.

However, despite all these miraculous technological advances, the annual rate of miscarriages—the unintentional loss of a pregnancy up to twenty weeks of gestation—in the United States has remained at the fairly constant level of 20 percent (or one in five pregnancies). Miscarriages—known in medical terminology as "abortions" or "spontaneous abortions"—account for 95 percent of all early losses.[5] They can occur so early in a pregnancy that they are virtually undetectable, or so late in the second trimester that they require extensive medical intervention either to deliver or to remove a significantly developed fetus.

Most miscarriages are caused by factors as varied as genetic and chromosomal defects, hormonal imbalances, uterine factors, immunological disorders, infections, injuries, and accidents. In over

50 percent of miscarriages, physicians cannot determine the specific cause.[6] There are few effective treatments for miscarriages and it is generally agreed that once a miscarriage begins there is very little that can be done to save the pregnancy. Because the rate of miscarriages increases with maternal age, as the trend toward women bearing children in their thirties and forties continues, the annual number of miscarriages in the United States is expected to increase.

In addition, the rate of ectopic pregnancies—in which the fertilized embryo implants outside of the uterus, usually in a fallopian tube where it must often be surgically removed to prevent internal hemorrhaging—has increased from 17,800 per year in the United States in 1970 to over 70,000 per year as of 1992.[7] This increase is probably due to a rise in the number of cases of pelvic inflammatory disease, the widespread use of IUDs (intrauterine devices) in the 1970s and '80s, DES (diethylstilbestrol) exposure, and the increased use of corrective tubal surgery for infertility.

Each year there are also an estimated 33,000 in vitro fertilization failures in the United States.[8] IVF, a fertility treatment procedure in which one or more fertilized embryos are transferred into a woman's womb, fails to result in a viable pregnancy in 40 to 80 percent of the cases where it is attempted, and although the failure of the embryo to implant is not defined as a pregnancy loss per se by the medical community, it is often indistinguishable emotionally from a pregnancy loss to those who undergo this procedure without success.

Many of the couples I have counseled are shocked by how much emotional weight an IVF failure carries. One woman I spoke with described the experience this way:

> *You only hear about the miracle babies, the big news stories about IVF babies being born to women who were infertile for ages. You don't want to think you might not be one of them. And it all gets*

so built up—the injections, the money, the scientific precision of the whole thing. You start to feel like "Wow! Its incredible what they can do these days, they've got it all under control." It might be a strange way to make a baby but you start to believe it's going to work, that it already has worked. You even get to see the embryos under the microscope! But when the pregnancy test came back negative I couldn't function for weeks afterwards. I just felt destroyed. And I was angry, too, because I felt like I wasn't expected to be so upset about it. After all, I hadn't ever really been pregnant. But I felt like I had been.

Including IVF failures, there are more than 700,000 pregnancy losses in the first twenty weeks of pregnancy each year in the United States alone, compared with 13,000 losses through stillbirth from the twentieth through thirty-eighth weeks of pregnancy, which makes early loss by far the most common of unintended losses.

The irony is that while the latest technologies have encouraged a very early attachment to new pregnancies and all that they may promise, the potential for early losses is still quite large. And while we have responded to the use of advanced technology by becoming more attached to our early pregnancies, there is little corresponding social recognition of that attachment. Partly because early pregnancy losses are still so common, they tend to be uniformly dismissed as relatively minor occurrences.

This lack of recognition often leads to embarrassment, shame and silence in those who lose early pregnancies, and to a failure to uncover the personal significance of the loss and the promise which this pregnancy held. Silence can lead to the repression of the trauma of the loss and can cause long delays in integrating the experience, which in turn can subtly affect one's view of life and self in detrimental ways. The emotional aftereffects of early losses are often hidden, not only from the rest of the world but from the would-be parents themselves.

This was certainly the case with Rebecca H.,* whose primary complaint when she entered treatment with me, was her inability to stop brooding about her ex-husband's departure several years prior. On some level, Rebecca realized that her preoccupation with her ex-husband's betrayal (he had left her for someone else) was unproductive. It left her little time, energy or enthusiasm for new relationships, or even to enjoy any aspect of her life. But she didn't feel she was capable of behaving differently. Neither of us had any idea that there was a connection between her stagnation and her long-buried feelings about a pregnancy and miscarriage she had had shortly before her marriage fell apart.

Almost a year after she began treatment, Rebecca told me the following dream:

> *I am swimming in a huge body of water. I don't know what it is . . . maybe a lake or something. I think it's bigger than a swimming pool but there's a concrete ledge to it that I'm holding on to. And then I'm under water and I see a baby floating down. I can't tell if it's dead or alive and so I keep trying to dive down to save it but I can't find it, I keep losing it. I can't see it. And then suddenly it's there again and when I try to get to it it disappears again. I'm getting frantic and scared and I'm afraid because I'm all alone and I'm calling for help but no one can hear me.*

Rebecca relates this dream in a surprisingly flat, detached manner. She is a tall, slender, dark-haired woman of forty years, who has a no-nonsense approach to life, owns her own business, devotes herself to her work and has little time or patience for introspection. Her tense, almost hostile expression is rarely softened by a smile. In the time we have been working together Rebecca has made it clear that she is in psychotherapy only because nothing else has worked to alleviate a host of stress-related physical prob-

* See note on page 7 concerning the names and identities of patients and interviewees.

lems which have plagued her for most of her adult life, many of which worsened immediately following her husband's departure and their eventual divorce.

She suffers from chronic back pain of unknown origin (for which she consults a chiropractor) and periodic abdominal pain, especially around ovulation. Laparoscopic surgery and ultrasonography have revealed no abnormalities—such as ovarian cysts—that might be causing her physical distress.

Despite her skepticism, Rebecca and I have developed a reasonably good working relationship: although she remains unconvinced that knowing more about her inner emotional life might help to alleviate some of her physical problems, she has obtained enough relief while in psychotherapy to keep at it for the time being. Being a person who finds it necessary to guard closely her tender feelings, she has managed to protect herself from dangerous exposure by denying that she has any real investment or interest in the process of self-discovery she is engaged in.

"And don't ask me what it means," said Rebecca after she told me the dream of the drowning baby. "Because I don't have a clue."

"I see," I said. "Well I wonder, then, why you remembered it and also why you thought to bring it here?"

"That's easy," she said with the hint of a grin. "Because you asked me if I ever remembered my dreams."

"That's true," I said, "I did. But what are *your* thoughts about the dream?"

She paused for a long time as I considered what, based on my knowledge of Rebecca to that point, my own interpretation of her dream would be. In the past few months we had been focusing on Rebecca's anger at her ex-husband and her apparently strong need to remain cold and unforgiving toward him. His abrupt departure had been devastating, and his announcement of an involvement with another woman was a profound betrayal of her trust in him. But the fact was that the marriage had been deteriorating for quite some time, and when she was honest with herself she couldn't help but admit that she, too, had often wished for an escape from what had seemed like a trap to her as well. However, her conviction that he was the only one at fault seemed to protect her from the even more devastating sense that she had failed him in some important way, which—for many reasons originating in her early childhood experience—was nearly intolerable to her.

In the previous session she had begun to express a deep sense of shame that she was not "good enough" and that perhaps her personal inadequacies had led to the breakup of her marriage. I suspected that the dream was related to this, that it might express her desperation in not being able to hold on to her husband, and the sense of responsibility she felt for his departure. I was considering how to suggest some of this to Rebecca when she finally spoke up.

"It's about my miscarriage," she announced.

Rebecca had never mentioned a pregnancy or miscarriage and I was surprised to hear her mention it now. Her only reference to children before had been to say that it was fortunate that she hadn't had any during her ten-year marriage, since the marriage had disintegrated. I wondered why the dream had surfaced now and why she was so certain that it referred to her pregnancy loss. She assured me that the miscarriage was of little significance to her and that she had long since put the incident behind her and "moved on with her life." But she couldn't explain why the dream had come up now, or why she was so certain it was about her miscarriage. Only after I began to question her closely about the details of the pregnancy loss did it dawn on her that the miscarriage had taken place on December 15, almost exactly two years prior. Though she seemed reluctant to discuss it, little by little, the story of the accidental pregnancy came out.

"I was shocked," she said. "By then we weren't even sleeping together. I mean *rarely*. He was always too busy avoiding me by working all the time."

Though she knew her husband Ron was strongly opposed to

having children and would probably be upset by the news, Rebecca found herself elated when the nurse told her over the phone that the blood test was positive.

"I was thirty-eight and I felt like I was too old to get pregnant. I had really given up on the whole idea of ever having a child. I couldn't see myself as a mother. But I felt like it proved I could do *something* right. If I was a failure as a wife at least I could have a baby."

Pleased as she was with the sense of competence her pregnancy inspired, Rebecca knew it would cause conflicts with Ron. They were arguing about the amount of time he spent working and how little time he seemed to want to spend with her. Because his views on having children had not wavered in the ten years of their marriage—he didn't want the strain, the disruption, the responsibility—she was fairly certain he would urge her to have an abortion.

"It was completely unreal. I kept expecting to get my period any day, even after the blood test. But then I started getting nauseated and exhausted and it began to seem a little more real. I couldn't believe it but I was starting to look at baby toys and clothes in the stores and I was staring at pregnant women. It must have been the hormones. I couldn't really imagine having an abortion even though that's exactly what I'd always thought I'd do if I ever got pregnant. So I guess I did a great job fooling myself. I started imagining that Ron might feel differently too and that maybe it would bring us closer together. He might even be more interested in spending time with me again . . . Ha! What a joke!"

When Rebecca told Ron about the pregnancy, they had one of the worst arguments they'd ever had.

"He accused me of getting pregnant on purpose, which was ridiculous because we'd both decided not to bother with birth control that night, and he was furious with me for not telling him the instant I found out. He said I was trying to manipulate him into keeping the baby and then—in his typically dramatic way—he jumped in the car and left. I didn't hear from him for days."

The day after Ron left, Rebecca started spotting. She also starting getting menstrual-type cramps which increased in intensity as the day went on. When she called her ob/gyn he told her to come into the office. He examined her and ordered a blood test to measure the level of HCG—the pregnancy hormone—in her system. Then he told her to rest in bed as much as possible and said his office would call her when the test results came in. She might or might not be miscarrying. Early miscarriages can mimic perfectly ordinary cramping and bleeding in the first trimester and are sometimes difficult to diagnose. She was told to limit her activities and to pay attention to how much she was spotting, and whether the color changed from brown to red. He told her that miscarriages were quite common in women her age[9] and that the older the mother, the greater the risk of pregnancy losses from chromosomal and other problems. There was not much to do but wait.

That night Rebecca's bleeding got worse and the cramps increased in intensity:

> *I knew the pain wasn't normal. I tried lying very still, holding my breath. I felt like if I could just not move, the cramping would let up and the bleeding would stop. I swore I really wanted the baby . . . I would take care of the baby, raise it on my own if I had to. The bleeding seemed to slow down some and the cramping stopped too and I fell asleep for a while. But then the cramps woke me up again a few hours later and they were really bad this time and I had to rush to the toilet and there was a lot of blood and clots and I don't know what else. When the doctor finally called me back he asked me what had passed out of me and he told me to come in the next day for an exam. He said he might have to do a D&C if the miscarriage wasn't "complete."*

As it turned out Rebecca did have to undergo a D&C (dilatation and curettage), a medical procedure which involves dilating the cervix and—usually under general anesthesia—scraping the contents of the uterus with a spoonlike instrument to ensure that no remnants of the pregnancy remain to cause further hemorraghing or possible infection. When miscarriages occur at twelve to twenty weeks' gestation a different but similar procedure is used, called a D&E (dilatation and evacuation), in which a suction pump is employed to remove the uterine lining and remnants of pregnancy. Both procedures are routinely performed as same-day surgery in the hospital. When Rebecca returned home from the hospital later that day, Ron had come home.

"When I told him what had happened he was real quiet," she told me. "He even apologized. But I know it was only because he felt guilty that he'd walked out on me like that. What else was new? He was *always* sorry after he did something inhuman . . . I guess I wasn't very nice either. I told the baby it could go if it wanted to. It might be better if it did. After he walked out the door I was so furious with him for being such a jerk . . . I didn't think it would really happen."

"Do you feel like you were responsible for the miscarriage?" I asked her.

"No," she said, after a short pause. "I blamed him. And I still do."

"Is that why you're still so angry with him?"

"Maybe," she said. "I'll never forgive him."

I thought of her dream of the water baby drowning. It was up to her to save it and in the dream she was failing.

"Maybe you can't forgive yourself, either," I suggested.

In the months that followed, Rebecca and I began to delve beneath the surface of her rage against her husband to uncover a profound sense of hurt in response to his withdrawal from her— both during her pregnancy and several months later, when he announced his involvement with another woman: a hurt which, as it turned out, had especially deep roots in the early emotional abandonments she experienced growing up.

Anger is not an uncommon cover for the pain of abandonment or neglect, especially when such abandonments occur in early life. It can be an overwhelmingly frightening experience for a vulnerable young child, whose very survival depends on the goodwill of the adults in her life, to be deserted. It is sometimes preferable to be angry rather than to be terrified.

Rebecca's mother had been clinically depressed, which prevented her from being a stable source of emotional nourishment for her growing daughter. From the time Rebecca was four, following the birth of her younger brother, until she was almost eight years old, her mother had been hospitalized for severe depression at least three times. When she was at home, her mother was quickly overwhelmed by the strain of caring for two young children and frequently retreated to the solitude of her bedroom, leaving Rebecca to care for her baby brother. Rebecca was highly critical of her mother—she saw her as weak, helpless, and incompetent—and she was still so enraged with her that she could hardly stand to speak of her.

Because her relationship with her mother had been so conflicted I was surprised that Rebecca's pregnancy seemed to hold such a positive value for her. Her hostility toward her own mother might easily have resulted in an unwillingness to embrace the role of motherhood, due to a fear of either repeating the neglect she had experienced as a child or of not being able to be an adequate mother herself. It is not unusual for women whose own experiences being mothered were unsatisfactory to be extremely fearful of pregnancy, childbirth or parenting.

Apparently, before she had become pregnant Rebecca, too, experienced these fears. Her change of heart upon becoming pregnant had been puzzling to her as well.

"I'm not the earth-mother type," she said. "As anyone who knows me can tell you. I'm just not. It just wasn't like me to be looking through baby catalogs and circling everything I wanted."

Something had happened during her brief pregnancy that had

significantly changed her feelings about motherhood. I suspected it had something to do with the discovery of her latent procreative abilities and an unconscious realization that having a baby of her own could provide her with the opportunity to be a different, more attentive mother than her own mother had been. In this way, she might be able to at least partially compensate for the deprivations she had endured as a child. Whether we are consciously aware of them or not, the babies we fantasize about express some of our deepest hopes and fears for our own lives.

To try to find out whether Rebecca was unconsciously seeking a reparation of her own childhood, I encouraged her to tell me everything she could about what she imagined this baby might have been like, and what her hopes had been for the kind of relationship they might have had.

"I don't know," she said. "I never thought about it that much... I might have imagined it was a girl . . . because I would have wanted a girl. But it seems ridiculous to think about it because I'll never know what it was."

Rebecca's miscarriage had taken place between the sixth and eighth week of pregnancy. A definitive gender identification is often impossible at such an early gestational age, which makes losses at this stage less tangible and harder to grieve. Uncertainty about the gender of a child does not prevent a woman or her partner from constructing numerous and detailed fantasies about the baby, however. Especially in cases where the loss has been preceded by a long struggle to conceive, or when the loss follows a long-planned and hoped-for pregnancy, the fantasies may be quite prominent although unconscious.

"It's hard thinking about who that baby might have been," I suggested.

"Not really," Rebecca said. "I just don't know."

That ended the discussion. But several weeks later, as if in response to my request to know more about her fantasy baby, Rebecca brought me yet another dream.

I am really pregnant, my stomach is huge. It feels gigantic. Then my point of view kind of changes and I can see inside my womb and there is a fully formed baby girl curled up inside, only she isn't a baby, she's a young girl about seven or eight years old with long dark hair just like mine. And I'm looking at her and it's really weird because all of a sudden I realize, "That's me!"

As we explored Rebecca's dream it became increasingly clear that the promise her baby held for her was the possibility to re-mother herself, and a great deal of her hidden despair over the loss of her pregnancy was related to the loss of that hope.

Rebecca had responded to her mother's frequent absences with anger, withdrawal and self-blame. As a child she had felt, as many children do, that she was in some way responsible for her mother's illness: that she was too demanding and needy and that her self-ishness was damaging to her mother. As a result she became high-ly attuned to her mother's moods and quite unaware of her own—except when her mother would leave for the mental hospital again and then she would feel panicky and agitated.

Eventually Rebecca's desperate longing for her mother would turn to anger, and even when her mother returned Rebecca would angrily withdraw from her. British psychoanalyst John Bowlby[10] says this is a typical pattern of response for young chil-dren who are separated from their mother. Protest, searching and depression frequently are followed by detachment and, if the dis-ruption in the parent–child bond is severe enough, an impairment in the child's ability to form new attachments to others in later life, causing them to become capable of only "anxious attachments" to others.

Rebecca's ability to form new attachments certainly had been severely limited following two significant events in her adult life: first, the miscarriage of her wanted pregnancy, and second, the loss of her marriage. Rebecca responded to Ron's moody departures with angry withdrawal, just as she had withdrawn in anger from her mother. In becoming pregnant, Rebecca had glimpsed the possibility of providing a more secure emotional environment for her own child and—by identification with that child-to-be—had seen the possibility for a different outcome for herself.

"I remember when I first found out I was pregnant," she said, "I had memories of going shopping with my mom and baking chocolate chip cookies. I guess I was looking forward to doing that with my little girl. Only *I* wouldn't get depressed and leave her."

"And when the baby died?" I asked.

"I was angry."

"At who?" I asked.

"At Ron, mostly. But I think I was angry at the baby, too, as crazy as that sounds. Maybe I felt like I deserved it."

"Why?"

"I don't know. I did something wrong. I screwed up."

"Like you did with your mom?" I asked.

"Yeah, I guess, " she said, as her eyes filled with tears. "Sometimes I feel like that baby was my only hope."

Losses never stand alone. New losses reverberate with the memories of old ones, bringing a new significance to each. We are constantly trying to make sense of our experiences, to make our lives coherent, to make what happens to us meaningful. When sudden, unexpected losses occur we have to struggle to make sense of them. They can threaten to overwhelm us with a sense of our own impotence until we come up with an explanation for why they occurred and how we can avoid having them happen to us again.

When parents leave suddenly with no explanation, when children are punished unfairly, when—as in the case of incest—their bodies are invaded by the adults they rely on to protect them, children make sense of these events by assuming they did something wrong and they try to be "better" so that these punishments won't be inflicted on them again. To assume that their own misbehavior is the cause gives them a crucial sense of control over an essentially chaotic situation.[11]

In much the same way, when a traumatic event occurs, there is a strong psychological need to provide one or more explanations for it. Often, these explanations are not fully conscious: they exist in the realm of unspoken beliefs about the nature of the world and the nature of one's self. Explanations for traumatic miscarriages may include the belief that the pregnancy loss was "caused" by a personal flaw of some kind. Unexpected losses may also lead to the conclusion that the world is an extremely hazardous place, or the belief that whatever is given will soon be taken away. We learn compelling lessons from our losses.

In Rebecca's case, the unconscious lesson learned time and time again—following her mother's repeated departures, the loss of her baby and the loss of her husband—was that because of some profound flaw in her, everyone she loved would abruptly leave her.

Rebecca realized she had lost hope in the future when she'd had her miscarriage and that her hopes for ever being content with her life had died then too. Shortly after her miscarriage, her ex-husband had moved out of the house. Although he asked about her health after the D&C, they had never talked about the pregnancy after the night of the big argument. It was as if it never happened—except that they both knew it had, and the silence about the loss of their baby became an impenetrable barrier between them. Neither of them ever referred to the baby's due date after the miscarriage, even though they had both known that it was close to the Fourth of July. But by then Ron had permanently moved out, and Rebecca said she had forgotten all about it. The miscarriage had taken place so early in her pregnancy that Rebecca had not told many people about it and the ones who did know never brought up the subject directly. They only asked how she was feeling, as if she had only been ill.

It was clear that Rebecca had minimized the impact of her miscarriage and had never really let herself experience the full impact of her despair when she lost her baby, a heartache which was exacerbated by an intense unconscious hope for reparation of her own past injuries. Just when she had finally gained the confidence that she had it in her to be a more adequate mother to her own child than her own mother had been to her, that confidence was shattered in the wake of her miscarriage—a loss which seemed to prove to her that she was unfit and inadequate after all. No wonder she was angry, and no wonder she displaced her self-loathing onto her husband.

Our work in therapy became harder from that point on. There were many days when she couldn't see the point of it all and seriously contemplated quitting. I often doubted myself whether Rebecca would have the fortitude to make the necessary fundamental shift in her worldview to see her own contribution to the problems in her marriage—specifically her hypersensitivity to any hint of abandonment by her husband. This was related to the difficulty she had tolerating the sense of vulnerability the important losses in her life evoked in her. I reminded her that the door to her sorrow had been opened from the first day she spoke about her lost child and that she now had an opportunity to continue to keep it open so that she could finally feel the full impact of the other important losses of her life—not only the loss of her marriage but the early and repeated loss of her mother's attention and affection. It was her choice, though: she could also choose to slam the door shut and remain protected but immobilized by her anger.

Unfortunately, profound psychological changes never seem to take place in an easily identifiable manner. One step forward is inevitably followed by even more steps backward or, worse yet, no apparent movement whatsoever. The process of internal change is so mysterious, in fact, that it is almost impossible to know for certain that changes are taking place until something happens to indicate that an important shift in attitude has already occurred.

That moment took place for Rebecca the day she brought in a photograph of her new baby nephew Jonathan, whose birth she had recently attended. We had talked about whether she really wanted to be there when her sister gave birth. At first she was repulsed by the idea and thought she might be physically ill at the sight of blood. Later we discovered that she was actually more afraid that attending the birth might arouse too much jealousy and pain for her to handle.

At the end of our previous session together, Rebecca had not yet decided what she was going to do. But she was beaming as she told me all the details about seeing her nephew being born and being the second person—after her brother-in-law—to hold him.

"I know I'm never going to be able to make up for what happened when I was kid. There's nothing I can do about it now, not even if I'd had the little girl I wanted. That promise of a happy childhood was broken a long time ago. But I can be there for Jonathan. It's kind of a new promise."

The losses of early pregnancy are all too easily forgotten, and in the deep silence surrounding these losses, it can be hard to gauge their influence on us. Some early losses are minor, relatively inconsequential events. Others are not. Everything depends on the context of the loss and how the loss is eventually interpreted. It is not abnormal to be able to brush off an early miscarriage, or even to see it as a *positive* sign: depending on her life circumstances, a woman may well regard an early loss as either a blessed escape from an undesired responsibility or even a positive sign that she and her partner are fertile. And some people, even when they are strongly attached to their lost pregnancies, are able to quickly reinvest whatever hopes and dreams their lost pregnancy represented into the next one.

By the same token, it also is not pathological to be affected by an early pregnancy loss for months or years afterward, as Rebecca was, or to have these seemingly minor occurrences exert considerable influence on us on a very deep level. This is especially true if some particularly compelling hopes and dreams were wrapped up in the lost pregnancy and there is no obvious alternative route for their fulfillment. Too often, because of the social taboos surrounding early pregnancy losses, people in this situation feel ashamed of their continued preoccupation with their early losses.

After a few months, Rebecca was reluctant to talk about the miscarriage she had experienced, fearing that others would view her as being abnormally obsessed by it. So she stopped speaking of it, and stopped thinking about it, forcing the memories away whenever they arose. But on a deeper level, the loss of her baby echoed the loss of her husband and the early loss of her mother's attention.

In order to make sense of our experiences, especially the traumatic ones, the aberrant ones that do not seem to "fit" with our view of the world, we tend to come up with plausible explanations for why certain things happen. Often, we are not fully aware of doing this. This is especially true when we are not encouraged to speak about our experiences openly. One couple I worked with had a miscarriage after years of infertility and had difficulty talking about their experience. Unfortunately, their unconscious explanation for this terrible loss, which I tried to challenge, was that they were fundamentally incompatible, and because they were unable to consciously deal with the question of their compatibility, they decided to separate. Another woman came to believe that her initial doubts about whether or not she wanted to become pregnant were the "cause" of the early loss she suffered, and could not trust herself to become pregnant again until she could be absolutely certain she wanted a child.

Some of the explanations we come up with about our unanticipated losses seem to substantiate our mistaken beliefs about the nature of the world and our place in it. For example if, on the basis of childhood experience, we tend to see the world as a cruel and unforgiving place, we might interpret the early loss of a wanted pregnancy as further confirmation of that view. Likewise, if we see ourselves as powerless and inevitably victimized by life, we might see this same loss as one more proof that we will never have any control over anything in life. Often, we are not even fully aware of the fundamental worldviews we hold; we simply act in accordance with them.

For Rebecca, the unexpected pregnancy seemed like her last chance to provide for a child what she had been deprived of herself: a stable, emotionally attentive mother. Her explanation for why this opportunity was taken away from her (which she was not fully aware of until she uncovered it in therapy) was that she was so inadequate that it "made sense" that her unborn baby, like her mother, would leave her. This fit with her distorted worldview—developed to explain her mother's frequent absences in childhood—that everyone she loved would eventually leave her due to her terrible and incurable flaws. Without her being fully aware of it, Rebecca's miscarriage was, in a sense, the final straw. It was definitive proof of the existence of these repulsive personal characteristics. After the miscarriage, Rebecca could not risk close involvement with anyone again. She knew exactly how it would end.

In the process of grieving for her vanished baby, though, Rebecca began to understand more fully what the loss had meant to her. She came to know the specific dreams she held for her baby and the promise that motherhood held for her, and she also became aware of her fundamental worldview: the belief that she was so flawed everyone she loved would eventually leave her. Once we were aware of how inadequate she felt, Rebecca and I could begin, together, to question the validity of this mistaken belief and to find evidence of its falsehood. There were many people she loved who had not abandoned her, and there were always people around who wanted to be with her, including me.

By speaking about her loss—and exploring and dispelling the mistaken way she had unconsciously interpreted it—Rebecca ultimately was able to see her miscarriage as something ill-fated and utterly beyond her control, and to risk reinvolvement in close relationships with others.

Breaking the silence surrounding significant early pregnancy losses, and becoming aware of how they may have been unconsciously understood, is the only way that mistaken beliefs about the world and oneself can be brought to light, and ultimately corrected. By remaining silent and unaware of our thoughts and feelings about these events, we risk explaining our losses to ourselves in ways that may tend to confirm these bleak and self-limiting worldviews. By uncovering the promise that a specific pregnancy holds, we can truly begin to let it go.

THREE

A Grief Delayed: Later Losses

I saw death in the bare trees, a deprivation. . .
The sun is down. I die. I make a death.

— SYLVIA PLATH[1]

ANISHED TO the waiting room of the maternity ward, Matthew sits stunned in his chair, oblivious to the gash on his forehead he received walking into a door after kissing his wife as she was being wheeled into the operating room for an emergency cesarean section. Sixteen hours of labor have passed with no sign of progress. And with each passing hour, Matthew has fought hard to contain his mounting anxiety. It hadn't taken this long with his first wife. The labor had been so short, so easy, the delivery so uncomplicated. Ten years ago this very month, in this very hospital, in this very maternity ward. So little had changed.

Except that at that time he had been trying to concentrate on an article on the New York Knicks in *Sports Illustrated* when the doctor finally entered the waiting room and Matthew rose to meet him.

> *"Your son is dead," [the doctor] said. "My son is dead,"*
> *[Matthew] thought. "He must take me for someone else. I have no*
> *son." He could no longer see out of his glasses, and he almost*
> *knocked over the doctor as he ran out of the room to find his wife.*
> *She was lying on the bed, rigid, with a face that expressed no emo-*
> *tion.[2]*

As he waits for the door to open once again, the only thing he is aware of is how incredibly dry his mouth is. He is gripping his chair, bracing himself for the news.

When the door opens at last the doctor isn't alone. The nurse beside him is carrying a tiny bundle in her arms. "Congratulations, *dad*. Here's your daughter," she says, handing him the sleepy new-born. As he holds the baby in his arms a wave of emotion hits him with such force that he is almost knocked off his feet and they have to guide him to his seat. He is laughing and crying at the same time and the nurse is a little alarmed. A short while later, she tells him it's time to take the baby away for her APGAR tests and he reluctantly hands the nearly weightless newborn over to her. "Don't worry, you'll see her soon," she says cheerfully as she walks away.

As soon as his daughter is taken from him Matthew breaks down. He is sobbing convulsively, panic-stricken that they will never bring her back. He tells himself he should pull himself together, that the baby will be fine, but he can't stop crying. A sin-gle thought occupies his mind: "My son is dead."

For ten years Matthew has not allowed himself to know that he is the father of a son who died at birth. Now it is hitting him with the all the force of a decade of unconsciousness. They are all wrong. He is not a *new* father. This miraculous daughter is his sec-ond child. Matthew is weeping uncontrollably now.

When a baby dies in utero at any time between twenty weeks' gestation and the time of delivery, it is considered stillborn. This approximate midway point of a typical thirty-eight to forty-week pregnancy is the point at which, in most states, a death certificate is legally required to be issued at the time of the baby's delivery. Before twenty weeks, no certificate is required since a death is not considered to have taken place.

Stillborn. Born still. The words evoke an image so disturbing that the impulse is to turn away. The moment of birth is supposed to be an exhilarating event. The squirming wet baby draws its first breath of air and then, screwing up its face, cries out to announce its arrival in the world. The moment of birth is the antithesis of death.

The idea of death before birth is almost too cruel to fathom. It is an offense against our belief in the cycle of life. With varying degrees of difficulty, we can come to accept the death of an elderly person, especially one who has lived a long, productive life: at some level we know that this is all that any of us can hope for. The moment of birth ordinarily transports us far from the bitter fact of our own mortality, but a stillborn baby brings the dark shadow of death into the delivery room.

Every year in the United States, approximately 60,000 to 70,000 fetal deaths (or stillbirths) take place between the twentieth and fortieth weeks of gestation,[3] although there is reason to believe that this number is underreported. This figure comprises close to 10 percent of the almost 700,000 early pregnancy losses each year due to miscarriage, ectopic pregnancy, and IVF failures.

The causes of stillbirth are numerous, ranging from problems with the position and function of the placenta or umbilical cord, to maternal illness or conditions affecting the pregnancy, to birth defects in the baby. One of the most common causes of stillbirth is the premature separation of the placenta from the uterine wall, called *abruptio placentae,* which causes vital oxygen and nutrients to be cut off from the in utero baby. Structural defects in the umbilical cord can also cause stillbirth. Occasionally the cord can become wrapped around the baby's neck either before or during delivery, or it may develop a kink or knot which restricts the flow of oxygen to the baby. If the umbilical cord prolapses—that is, comes out of the uterus before the baby does—the baby's oxygen supply may also become severely restricted. The placenta can also become nonfunctional due to maternal illnesses such as hypertension, diabetes, lupus, preeclampsia, and infections.

Cigarette smoking and the use of cocaine can also restrict the flow of oxygen through the placenta. In other cases, malformations in the baby—chromosomal or nonchromosomal—can cause stillbirths. Autopsies are frequently performed to try to pinpoint the cause of death, but in more than 50 percent of the cases no definitive cause is found, making the event even more difficult to endure.

In cases where the baby's death prior to delivery is suspected by the absence of movement or a heartbeat, an ultrasound exam can confirm the diagnosis of in utero fetal death. In the past, although fetal death may have been suspected, without the use of fetal monitoring or ultrasonography—which provides a view of the baby's beating heart on the sonogram screen—such knowledge often was not absolutely certain until the baby was delivered. Also, the number of fetal deaths at twenty to forty weeks' gestation has decreased, from 14.2 per 1,000 live births in 1970 to 7.3 per 1,000 in 1991.[4] This may be due to the widespread use of fetal monitoring and the increased number of cesarean sections performed when fetal distress is detected or suspected.

As a result, many fetal deaths today are detected prior to delivery, and parents often are given the option of having labor induced rather than having to wait—sometimes days or weeks—for labor to begin naturally. Modern technology has thus made an almost unthinkable experience a reality: carrying and giving birth to a baby who is known to be dead.

A woman who discovered her baby had died during labor looks back on her experience:

> *After they give birth, and even for years afterwards, a lot of women talk about the experience of labor and delivery. It's like there is this strong need to do so for some reason—like talking about the battles you fought and won. But no one ever talks about what it's like to give birth to a baby who is stillborn.*

Another woman describes her experience this way:

> *I felt like the pain of labor and delivery was much worse and I think it lasted a lot longer than it would have otherwise because I knew I was going through all this struggle for nothing. The only thing I had to look forward to was a dead baby.*

Anaïs Nin[5] writes of the difficulty in giving birth to a baby known to be dead:

> *. . . a part of me did not want to push out the child . . . a part of me lay passive, did not want to push out anyone, not even this dead fragment of myself, out in the cold, outside of me . . . to be lost, lost, lost.*

For some, however, the death of the baby is not discovered until the baby is delivered. When this happens, the news of the baby's death can have the emotional impact of an act of terrorism. One mother describes discovering at the moment of birth that her baby was dead:

> *I think we were both stunned for days afterward. We didn't know what had hit us.*

For most parents, the intense ambivalence characteristic of the first months of pregnancy becomes less prominent in the later months, as they—especially the mother—are forced to turn their attention to the more immediate concern: that of providing for the arrival of a creature who visibly protrudes from the mother's abdomen, whose kicks are growing increasingly strong, and whose heartbeat seems to compete in strength with that of the mother. It is at this time that the parents-to-be, more convinced of the actual existence of their newcomer, begin in earnest to prepare for the baby's presence and to take their role as parents more seriously. As the psychological adaptation to parenthood progresses, they begin to take concrete steps to prepare for the arrival of their child. The carefully decorated and furnished nursery and layette are indications of their progress in accepting parental responsibilities and of their growing belief in the actual existence of their baby. A woman with a newborn describes how she felt just prior to her baby's birth:

> *Maybe no one ever feels completely prepared for the arrival of their baby, but we had received so many gifts at the baby shower and I had all the teddy bears lined up on the bureau and the crib all made up with new flannel sheets. I didn't completely believe that I was really going to be using the hand-knit blanket that was packed in the bags I was ready to take to the hospital. I kept trying to imagine what it was going to be like to have someone wrapped in it.*

Few parents, of course, feel fully prepared for the major event that is about to take place in their lives. Most struggle with fears about their adequacy as parents and their ability to adapt to the rigors of parenthood. It is not uncommon for prospective parents to have anxiety dreams in the latter half of pregnancy, such as those one woman had during the last trimester of her pregnancy:

> *I was having recurring dreams that the baby's clothes were gone and I couldn't find the diapers and I keep looking through the draw-*

ers in the nursery and I can't find all kinds of things I thought were there. It was really frustrating and I would wake up really scared.

A man whose wife was about to give birth any day describes the anxiety that surfaced in his dreams just prior to his son's birth:

I had this ridiculous dream about not being able to find my car keys to drive my wife to the hospital. And then she was getting angry with me and I was trying to make a call to get some help and I couldn't get the right number or the phone wouldn't work. I kept trying to get it to work and I just couldn't.

As the growing baby begins to take up more and more physical space inside the mother—actually rearranging the position of her internal organs—the mother has to make some significant changes in her day-to-day life to accommodate to the physical demands of pregnancy and childbirth. The need to put aside her own desires for the sake of her baby's health and well-being can give rise to unconscious (or conscious) resentment of the baby—especially if the father (in his biologically more privileged position) is perceived as not making similar sacrifices.

Moreover, the idea of giving birth to what appears to be a disproportionately huge infant is almost universally an overwhelming prospect for mothers. The fear—either conscious or unconscious—of being split open during childbirth or dying during either labor or delivery is a very real concern for many women, perhaps originating in an awareness that in earlier times death in childbirth was far more common than it is today. The prospect of self-annihilation, either physical or psychological, makes preparing for childbirth a formidable psychological task for women and may contribute to an intense sense of guilt if—as in the case of stillbirth—only the mother survives the process of labor and delivery.

The psychological preparation for childbirth is termed "psychic gestation" by Italian psychoanalyst Sylvia Vegetti Finzi,[6] who maintains that "psychic gestation and physical gestation proceed separately" depending, in large part, on the particular psychological makeup of the mother, whether the baby is a wished-for child, and what the mother's life circumstances are at the time she becomes pregnant. She points out that in some very rare, and usually sensationalized, cases, psychic gestation never takes place, and when this happens the woman gives birth saying she *never knew she was pregnant*. In such cases, the mother finds the idea of her pregnancy so intolerable that she manages to repress all conscious awareness of her own bodily processes. But for most women, by the time they enter the second half of their pregnancies they have found a way to "bridge the gap between the psychic and corporeal" and are actively engaged in finding concrete ways to accommodate and provide for the new life—both physically and emotionally.

In this second half of the pregnancy the baby is often already considered to be a member of the family and—especially if its gender is known—may already have a name. The widespread use of prenatal diagnostic testing techniques such as amniocentesis and ultrasound monitoring, along with an overall decrease in the number of fetal deaths between twenty and forty weeks' gestation in the past two decades, leads parents to regard the birth of a healthy infant as virtually guaranteed. This tends to encourage them to begin their relationship with their babies while they are still in utero.

The death of a baby after so much psychic gestation has taken place can be a devastating blow to a couple's identity as parents, and often leaves them with the irrational but almost unshakable conviction that they have failed at the most fundamental parental task of all: safeguarding the life of their child. The mother of a stillborn baby who died in utero of unknown causes puts it this way:

> *I felt I did something wrong. I wasn't fit to be a good mother, I was too selfish and had too many complaints about the discomforts of my pregnancy. I wasn't a good enough mother and that's why she died.*

Her husband has another "explanation":

I thought maybe I hadn't been involved enough in my wife's pregnancy and that if I'd been more supportive maybe she would have felt more relaxed and the baby wouldn't have died.

In a series of in-depth interviews, many of them very heartfelt, Matthew told me the story of his son's stillbirth twenty years before and the impact it had had on his life. When Matthew's first wife, Mary Beth, was pregnant she quit her job and spent virtually all of her time preparing for the baby's arrival. By the time she went into labor, not only had she made sure that the nursery was decorated and fully supplied with teddy bears and baby toys, but she had even finished sewing a whole wardrobe of baby clothes for the new arrival. Everything was neatly arranged and ordered. Not a diaper pin was out of place. After the baby died, Mary Beth, who had not been allowed out of the hospital to attend the burial, held her own funeral when she returned home. She buried all the clothes and toys that she had so lovingly prepared. "For her," Matthew told me, "the baby's death was absolutely catastrophic."

The sudden, unexpected death of his son was a catastrophe for Matthew as well. It was like a bomb, the full impact of which he only really began to feel ten years later, the day his daughter was born.

"We never knew what happened. The doctor said the baby was a 'starved baby.' Mary Beth did smoke cigarettes while she was pregnant, but we didn't know then what the dangers were," Matthew explains. "The baby was alive the day before she was delivered. I expected to hold a live baby in my arms."

Although he was not as involved as his wife in the preparations of the nursery, Matthew's psychic gestation for his child had manifested itself in his increased commitment to a new teaching appointment and the greater sense of responsibility he felt to provide for the family financially. His preparations for fatherhood were in keeping with the conventional expectations of adulthood as defined by his family and his culture: First you get married, then you get a secure job, then you have your children. When he got his tenure-track teaching position at a private college, Mary Beth stopped taking birth control pills and they waited for the inevitable to happen.

At some unconscious level, however, Matthew may well have had deeper conflicts about becoming a father. For many years he and his father had been estranged. His father, an Irish Catholic immigrant and New York City cop, was an old-country patriarch who ruled his family with his fist. He viewed Matthew's mother essentially as a household servant, whose own needs and desires were not seriously considered. He was especially hard on Matthew and his brother, the only boys in the family. When Matthew misbehaved his father beat him "for his own good." Once, when Matthew was expelled from high school, his father kicked him so severely that he cracked Matthew's ribs. For many years after that, Matthew believed he had deserved this brutality. He both hated and feared his father, but underneath it all he longed for his father's approval and affection. The fear that by becoming a father himself he might inadvertently recreate this tragic relationship may have lurked just below the surface of his consciousness when his wife Mary Beth gave birth to their stillborn son.

It was a shock to Matthew to hear the doctor say his son was dead. Not having known the baby's gender prior to birth made the news that he was the father of a son, and that his son was dead, simply too much to comprehend. "I have no son," he thought. "They must be mistaken. I have no son." And when the doctor suggested that Matthew might want to see the baby, to see how perfectly formed he was, Matthew refused.

"Perfectly formed and dead," was his response. "I don't need the nightmares."

Matthew bought a casket the size of a shoe box and attended his son's funeral in a kind of dissociated state—unable to focus, unable to feel, unable to absorb the significance of what was happening.

> *I'm at the graveside now with two friends. The priest is praying. My mind and heart are dry and my tongue is stuck to the roof of my mouth. I'm not sure I want to but even if I do I can't get out the "Amen" that I think they are all waiting for me to pronounce. I feel an enormous relief when I hear them continue without me. As the priest sprinkles holy water on the casket and they lower it into the ground, I think that if I were an onlooker off to the right on the hilltop, I would assume that a group of men had gathered in a symbolical ritual to bury a tin of Anacin.[7]*

No one at the hospital offered counseling or suggested that he and his wife might benefit from psychotherapy. In fact, as is still quite typical, after the initial supportive phone calls everyone around them acted as if *nothing had happened,* and they expected Matthew and Mary Beth to forget about it too, to get on with their lives, maybe have another baby. Everyone, including medical personnel, seemed embarrassed and uncomfortable and wanted to avoid talking about what had happened.

In a study conducted in 1968, British psychologist S. Bourne[8] produced statistical evidence demonstrating that family doctors are remarkably reluctant to know or remember anything about their patients who have experienced stillbirths. Stillbirth seems to be an event which, even to this day, in the words of psychologist Emmanuel Lewis is "by common consent, cloaked in secrecy and by its nature seems unreal."[9] And when there is no tangible person to mourn, it is more difficult to come to terms with the loss.

"We didn't talk about it afterwards," Matthew told me, looking back. "We never knew anyone else who lost a baby like that . . . we felt we were the only ones it ever happened to . . . we felt really ly isolated and alone. We both did a lot of drugs—smoked a lot of dope; it was just too painful to talk about. I see now that was our way of coping." Two years after the stillbirth the marriage broke up. "The stillbirth isn't what caused our breakup. It drove us further and further apart. It was a bad marriage and the stillbirth made it worse. She was right to leave me. Everything revolved around me. I didn't give a damn about what she wanted. I was a terrible husband."

Several years after he was divorced, Matthew got involved with his current wife, Suzanne. Matthew's father, though initially opposed to the relationship because of his objections to the divorce, was softening his attitude toward both of them, and by the time they announced their engagement was eager to welcome Suzanne into the family. Matthew was so encouraged by the change in his father's attitude that he began to hope that an upcoming Christmas visit would bring the reconciliation with his father that he had secretly wished for all his life. But shortly before Christmas that year, Matthew's father died. Matthew went into a tailspin. He wept bitter tears, not only for the loss of his father but also, perhaps more importantly, for the lost opportunity to make peace with him.

When he returned home after his father's funeral, Matthew's behavior became increasingly more self-centered and uncompromising. Worse yet, he seemed unconcerned about the pain he was causing his new wife, Suzanne. "I realized I was in trouble," Matthew says, "when I saw the hurt in her eyes. It just came to me that here I was hurting the person who loved me most in the world. There was something wrong with me. I was on the verge of destroying my second marriage. I needed help."

Help came in the form of psychotherapy where, he told me, he was eventually able to recognize how much his own behavior as a husband was the result of an identification with his sometimes tyrannical and violent father and to stop seeking revenge for the brutal punishments he had received as a child.

The tendency of those who were abused as children to become abusive themselves is a commonly observed phenomenon. The psychological mechanism underlying this tendency, however, is not well understood. One theory is that the victimized child—especially if it is a boy—learns that all relationships are based on a perpetrator-victim dynamic, and will tend to seize the first opportunity to assume the more powerful position as abuser.

For boys, an unconscious identification with a father who abuses his authority and power in the family makes assuming a fatherly role that is *not* abusive quite problematic. In Matthew's case, the turning point came when he found he no longer hated his father but could see him as a human being who had not intentionally set out to hurt him. This realization freed him to choose a different path for himself. He began to treat his new wife Suzanne as he had often wished his father had treated his mother and himself: with a great deal more respect and consideration. "I realized I no longer needed to be in therapy," Matthew told me, "when I no longer hated my father."

When Suzanne became pregnant Matthew, though anxious, was an extremely involved and attentive husband. And during the sixteen long hours of labor he was with her every moment. He wanted to be with her in the operating room when they performed the cesarean section, but it was against hospital policy. As they wheeled her into surgery, Suzanne told Matthew that she never would have made it that far without him.

But all that time he had been with her, easing her fears, encouraging her, cheering her on, Matthew was aware of a growing panic inside him. From the moment they had walked through the hospital doors he had the unnerving feeling that he was about to reexperience the horror of his son's death ten years before. "Oh God, not again! I can't believe this!" he thought as Suzanne's labor failed to progress. "Not again!"

So a tremendous flood of relief swept over him when the smiling nurse appeared with the bundle and he held his daughter in his arms. When the nurse took his newborn daughter from him and he started sobbing uncontrollably, he thought at first it was the stress of Suzanne's long labor. But it scared him, too, because he knew something much deeper was happening and he didn't know what it was.

The Diagnostic and Statistical Manual of Mental Disorders (*DSM IV*) defines posttraumatic stress disorder[10] as following exposure to an extreme traumatic stressor (including the death of a family member or "close associate") with characteristic symptoms of intense fear, persistent involuntary reexperiences of the trauma (commonly known as flashbacks), numbing of general responsiveness and increased anxiety (often in the form of sleep disturbances). Exposure to "triggering events," those that "resemble or symbolize the trauma," often cause "intense psychological distress."

Recovering from the shock of a traumatic event seems to require reintegrating the experience; otherwise, the trauma remains deeply repressed and split off from conscious awareness. In this regard, the typical symptoms of PTSD (initial numbness followed by intense anxiety, flashback experiences, nightmares, and distress "triggered" by similar situations) may be seen as the mind's way of initially protecting itself from an overwhelming experience, then progressively reintroducing memories of it, so that it can eventually be reintegrated into consciousness. If the environmental circumstances are unfavorable to remembering the trauma, however—either because there is no support for remembering it or because remembering it may threaten the person's sense of safety in the world—the emotional processing of the trauma can be delayed for months or sometimes years. In other words, the person's full reaction to the trauma does not take place until it is safe to do so.

After his breakdown in the hospital waiting room, Matthew

grew so fearful for his daughter's safety that he couldn't sleep at night. He kept having to get up to check on her, and even that wasn't enough to reassure him sufficiently to let him get a good night's sleep. The triggering event that had instigated this intense anxiety was the coincidence of his daughter's being born in the same month, in the same town, and the same hospital where his son had been born and died ten years earlier. In addition, Suzanne had difficulties nursing, and the baby cried all the time, apparently because she was not getting enough food. In Matthew's mind, she was starving: just as his son had apparently starved in the womb.

Matthew told me that it was his severe anxiety about his daughter's safety that had sent him back to psychotherapy, where he learned to separate the death of his son from the birth of his daughter. And it was there that, after a ten-year delay, he began to mourn the loss of his son. The conscious awareness of his son's death did not give him nightmares, as he had feared viewing the body would. Instead, it made it possible for him to begin to sleep again.

When his daughter, Alice, was two years old, Matthew experienced another flashback to his son's death. The family was on a summer vacation in France when they were run off the road by a speeding driver. They were badly shaken but physically unharmed. The next day, they turned on the television to hear that a terrible car accident had taken place not far from where they were staying. Fifty-six people had been killed, including forty-six children from underprivileged families who had been on their way to camp.

When Matthew saw the miniature wooden caskets on the television he involuntarily reexperienced the death of his son. "The doors of my memory opened so wide," he later wrote in an eloquent article on the incident, "that I was thrust involuntarily through the corridor of time to an event that had taken place twelve years earlier. My former wife and I are walking through the

doors of the hospital. She is nine months pregnant and in labor...
The doctor tells me my son is dead."[11]

Matthew's daughter, Alice, is now sixteen years old. He tells me
that today, just before I called him, he was riveted to the news
accounts of a recent explosion of a U.S. airliner en route from
New York to Paris. No one survived. This is what he says:

> *I'm sure I still think more about the possible death of my daugh-*
> *ter than other people do about their children. I can tell you that I*
> *reacted to this airplane being blown up much worse than anyone I*
> *know. I sat in front of the TV the first day and I cried my eyes out.*
> *Sixteen of those kids are just like my daughter. They're the same*
> *age, they're in the French Club, just like she is. I immediately saw*
> *that it could have been her. I'm not saying that's the only reason I*
> *was crying. I was crying for those poor parents with whom I can*
> *identify and I was feeling desperately sorry for.*

Only when his daughter was safely in his arms could Matthew
let himself become aware of the horrifying fact that he was the
father of a son who died at birth. Only then could he begin to
grieve the loss of the little boy he never knew, and perhaps the loss
of the opportunity to raise a son in the presence of a tender father.

Matthew says his daughter has helped him come to grips with
the reality of his son's death. When she was six years old she ques-
tioned her parents closely about whether either of them had any
children in their previous marriages. Matthew told her about the
baby who had been born dead and was buried in a nearby ceme-
tery. Without telling anyone, Alice located her brother's grave and,
finding it overgrown, clipped the grass with a pair of scissors. This
heartfelt act further helped Matthew find the courage to face the
hard reality of his son's death.

Late-term pregnancy losses often carry with them an undeni-
able reality that earlier losses do not. The loss of a fully formed, vis-

ible, touchable child often is so sudden and so overwhelmingly traumatic that its impact is similar to that of a catastrophe—a train wreck, a fatal explosion. Memory loss of various aspects of the event, and emotional numbing, are common aftereffects. So are nightmares, and flashbacks, like the ones that Matthew had.

The initial numbing that occurs seems to be the mind's way of coping with a trauma that threatens to shatter it. Slowly, as one's equilibrium is regained, little snatches of memory start to come back, like tiny puzzle pieces that have to be reassembled.

This reconstructive work is often facilitated by seeing, touching, holding and taking photographs of the baby who died. It is also assisted by funerals, memorial services and other ceremonies which—by making the event public—tend to underline the reality of the death and allow grieving to begin.

Talking about exactly what happened, and eventually coming to the point where a detailed story can be told about the circumstances surrounding the loss, allows integration of the trauma into conscious awareness rather than leaving it stuffed into the closet of the unconscious where it can continue to inspire nightmares.

It has been said that mourning is like having a pool of grief you need to drink dry. You don't know how long it will take to get to the bottom; you just need to keep coming back to visit and drink a little bit more each time you do. One of the surest signs that the pool is diminishing is the ability to speak out loud about your loss, to identify yourself as the parent of a baby who died.

After almost twenty years, Matthew finally got to the bottom of his pool. It was then he could finally bring himself to say that he is the father of two children—one living and one who died at birth.

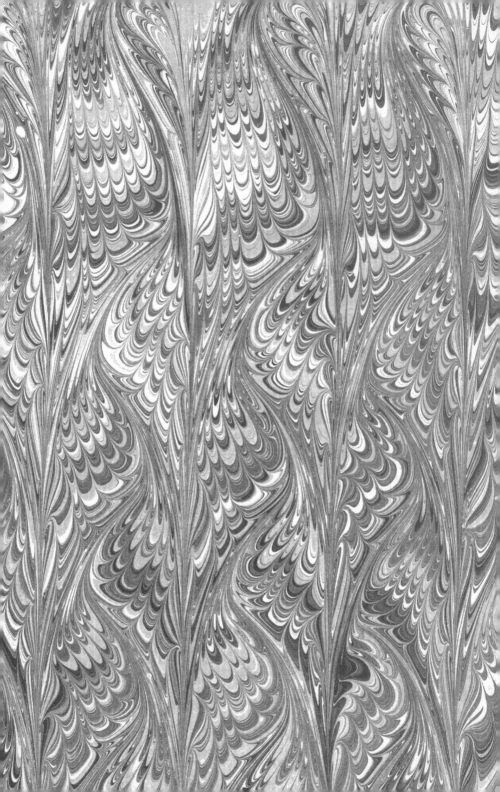

The Dilemma of Choice: Abortion—Elective, Genetic, and Multifetal Reductions

Two roads diverged in a yellow wood,
And sorry I could not travel both
And be one traveler . . .

—ROBERT FROST[1]

It feels dangerous to speak publicly about abortion. Unless it is merely to state one's allegiance to either the "pro-choice" or "pro-life" sides of the debate, the topic remains a deeply held taboo. And yet, between 1.52 and 1.6 million abortions (or 25 percent of the 6 million annual pregnancies)[2] are performed in the United States every year. Although the absolute number and the rate of abortions among women aged fifteen to forty-four has declined somewhat in the 1990s, by 1996 almost half of all women in that age group in the United States had had at least one abortion. This is a little known and rather staggering statistic.

It is not that surprising that the facts about the numbers of abortions performed in the United States are not well known. We are, after all, in the midst of a war over the legal right to abortion in this country and the heated, highly polarized struggle is dominated by strong voices on either side, each side eager to refute the other. Accusations of heartlessness, brutality and inhumanity are hurled through the air as those in the middle run for cover. In a war, there is no neutral zone. You're either for or against us, each side claims. Choose your side.

Unfortunately, what gets lost in all this are the voices of the many millions of women who, at some point in their lives, have chosen to terminate their pregnancies rather than carry them to term, each of whom made that decision in highly specific circumstances. What gets obscured by the intense ideological and legislative battle is that abortion is a difficult choice emotionally, morally and spiritually for many, if not most, women. And in the current political atmosphere, to speak the truth about one's own experience—both the positive and the negative sides of abortion—is to risk being condemned as a traitor by either side, or sometimes both.

In my practice I have known a number of women (and men, as well) for whom the psychological consequences of abortion were surprisingly long-term. There are those who believe that the depth of their grief over the loss of their offspring is inappropriate or even pathological because, according to many pro-choice supporters, abortion is a simple, common medical procedure (particularly when it takes place in the first trimester) with few, if any, profound psychological consequences.

I have also known others for whom the decision to have an

abortion, along with a conscious acceptance of responsibility for
that decision, has marked an important maturational turning point
in their lives. And these people have struggled with intense feelings of shame about their decisions, primarily because of the equa-
tion of abortion with murder by extremists on the pro-life side.

In our haste to make generalizations about the experience of
abortion for use as political ammunition, we forget that the experience itself, like any life experience, is neither black nor white:
neither wholly positive nor completely negative. Every abortion,
like every pregnancy, has an individual context and a particular,
personal meaning. Until we appreciate the individual life and the
context in which the decision was made, we cannot fairly judge
the morality of the decision. And until those who choose abortion
are free to uncover its psychological significance (without fear of
condemnation from either side of the political debate), it will continue to be very difficult for them to come fully to terms with the
emotional repercussions of their choices.

The three cases I discuss in this chapter demonstrate the
immense psychological and moral challenge that the decision to
end a pregnancy entails. The circumstances of the three abortions
are quite distinct: the age differences are large, the timing of the
abortions varies widely, and the women's reasons for choosing to
have an abortion were quite different. But for all three women, the
political controversy surrounding abortion was an obstacle that
prevented them from having full access to their own reactions, thus
complicating and delaying their recovery. The first case concerns a
long-delayed emotional reaction to an early elective abortion, the
second relates to second-trimester genetic abortion and the final
one describes the experience of a multifetal reduction.

Patricia was a young woman in her early twenties when she first
entered treatment with me. She reported feeling despondent following a recent breakup with her boyfriend, with whom she had

been deeply in love, but who she felt had misled her into believing that the feeling was mutual. Patricia had followed Stephen to Chicago from her home in California, because she thought that moving in with him was the first step toward marriage and, despite the fact that she had only known him for a little over three months, she felt ready for that commitment. However, once they were living together, Stephen seemed to become increasingly irritable and self-absorbed. When she became pregnant the tension between them escalated. They had been using the rhythm method of birth control, she said, and had miscalculated her fertile time of the month. The use of such an unreliable method of birth control may have indicated a desire on her part to become pregnant in an attempt to ensure the stability of the relationship.

A small, delicately pretty young woman who looked significantly younger than her twenty-four years, Patricia was extremely anxious. She spoke quickly and without any pauses, jumping from one pressing concern to another, laying out the story of her despair and berating herself at every turn.

"I should have known when I agreed to move all the way out there with him things would change. I mean, he said he was *totally in love* with me. He was so sweet. And romantic. He was a painter. A very good painter but he didn't believe in himself. He was very moody . . . temperamental. He used to like to do sketches of me all the time. He said he was making sketches for a portrait of me he was going to paint. That never happened!"

"Why not?" I asked.

"I don't know. He made a lot of promises. God, I was such an idiot to believe him! He'd had so many girlfriends. But I thought I was different, I was going to be the one he was going to finally settle down with. You know what hurts? What really hurts the most is how when we first got together he would talk about how much he wanted to have children with me, how he'd never met anyone like me and he'd never thought he wanted kids before. And he'd talk about how he wanted a boy and a girl. And we'd lay in bed and think up silly names for them. And then . . . then when I got pregnant . . . of course it was an accident because God knows I wasn't ready for it . . . but once it happened . . . part of me thought 'God, this is great!'"

"And what did he say when you told him?" I asked.

"He didn't say anything at first and I remember he turned away from me and he said, 'I *told* you I wasn't ready to be a father. I was . . . it was incredible! I knew it wasn't good timing but . . . and it's true *I* wasn't really ready either but since we had been talking about maybe getting married once we both had decent jobs . . . before then I hadn't really even thought about an abortion. All of a sudden it seemed like the best option. He didn't even have a job. I was supporting him! But just the way he said it was so . . . 'I told you I wasn't ready,' like it was my fault or something. Or like he thought I was lying, trying to trick him into marrying me or something. He was just so . . . cold. After all that talk about our beautiful babies. And then, and this is what really got me—" she paused, on the verge of tears "—after I had the it . . . the abortion . . . he did go with me to the clinic, thank God, and he waited for me and he drove me home, but when we got back to the apartment he just dropped me off at the door and said he had to go somewhere! And I was all alone in bed and it really hurt. I was in a lot of pain afterwards, cramping and stuff and I was scared. And he came home really late that night and he—" she was crying now and it was hard for her to speak "—he didn't even . . . he didn't even ask how I *was!*"

This was the turning point for Patricia. Though she had been willing to do more than her fair share to make the relationship work because she "loved him so much," that night she realized how alone she really was in the relationship and how one-sided things were. That night she decided to leave him and return to California.

In our sessions together we talked about what had led Patricia to fall for a man as self-involved as Stephen had been, and very little about the details of her abortion, how she had made the decision and what she had felt about the whole experience. Instead, most of our talk focused on her family experiences growing up.

Patricia and her three siblings had been raised by a financially strapped mother whose husband had long since abandoned the family physically and emotionally and who only intermittently provided financial support for (or expressed any interest in) his four children. Patricia, the model child, was the second to the oldest. Her older sister had abdicated the role of mother's helper and became heavily involved in the drug scene in high school, and her two younger brothers (less than two years apart in age) were held back for several grades and ended up dropping out of school.

Patricia, by contrast, was the good child, her mother's "savior," as she put it. She worked hard at school and helped her mother—who worked full-time—with the cooking and cleaning at home. When one of her siblings got in trouble, it was Patricia her mother turned to for comfort and consolation. Patricia worked hard to try to alleviate the burdens her siblings' behavior and her father's absence placed on her mother, but she could never completely escape the unconscious fear that her very existence was a major factor in her mother's misery.

In her teenage years, Patricia had a number of boyfriends in both junior and senior high school. Because she was so attractive, she tended to be one of the most sought-after girls at school despite the fact that she was somewhat aloof. The pattern in these relationships always seemed to be the same. At first she was worshipped by the young man, who did everything in his power to win her over. Then, slowly things would change. Eventually, it seemed to her, she was doing everything in her power to hold on to the relationship while the boyfriend became less and less interested in continuing it. In the end, the boy would break things off and she would be left once again, brokenhearted.

At an unconscious level, Patricia's choice of relatively narcissistic partners—ones who viewed her mainly as a means to their own ends—seemed to stem from a compulsion to repeat[3] (and perhaps try to alter) the abandonment she had experienced by her father. In another way, choosing such partners served to strengthen her identification with her "victimized" mother. But for some reason, Stephen's indifferent response to the announcement of her pregnancy opened her eyes to the treacherous course she was following. Had she chosen to have the baby against Stephen's wishes she would have followed perfectly in her mother's entrapped footsteps.

In the course of therapy we talked a great deal about Patricia's anxieties about being able to end a relationship for her own benefit. It was something quite different from what she had done in past relationships and a sharp contrast to what her own mother had done in her marriage to her father. Though her mother had been unhappy in the marriage and desperately wanted to leave, it seemed each time she felt ready to do so she got pregnant again. At that time her options once she became pregnant were limited—the state she was living in had not legalized abortion, and she had been afraid to seek out an illegal one.

Patricia's decision to have an abortion seemed to stem from a firm resolve to free herself from a relationship which was depleting rather than enriching her. And the fact that she had taken an action which had not been available to her own mother made her feel, on the one hand, as if she were vindicating her mother and, on the other, a little guilty for surpassing her mother. But on the whole, Patricia expressed tremendous relief about having ended her pregnancy, recognizing that she would not have been able to support a child on her own, nor tolerated staying in the relationship with Stephen only for the sake of the child. She had serious doubts, in fact, about whether Stephen would have provided any support for her and the baby given his attitude about fatherhood. Because the abortion had taken place in a context in which

Patricia was beginning to break out of the self-limiting patterns of past relationships, her decision seemed to both of us to be a very positive sign.

Over the next few months, as she explored the benefits of her decision to end the relationship with Stephen and to address her less conscious fear of not being entitled to more fulfilling relationships, the depression and anxiety which had brought her into therapy began to lessen. Not long after she started a new relationship with a man who seemed genuinely more attentive and less self-involved than her past boyfriends, Patricia decided to end therapy.

The termination of psychotherapy is often a tricky business. There are, of course no clear guidelines, no preordained rules about when the work one has set out to do in therapy is completed, and the passage of time alone offers no answers. And of course, no one ever completely finishes that work. What throws a monkey wrench into the whole business is that there are always unconscious forces at work and psychotherapy is arduous and sometimes uncomfortable. It's not easy to set aside the time and money to take a good look at yourself for an hour (or more) a week. It can seem like a huge self-indulgence, or worse, a worthless folly. It takes time and effort to sort out these factors and arrive at a decision about when to end therapy that makes sense. Ending therapy abruptly usually does not allow for that to happen.

When Patricia announced that our current session was to be our last, I tried to point all of this out to her. But she said she felt so much better that she couldn't rationalize spending the money to continue something she didn't really need anymore. We left the door open for her to return at some point in the future if she wished, and then she was gone.

The next time I heard from Patricia was six years later. She was married to the man she had met at the time she ended therapy. She was thirty years old and she had been trying to get pregnant for almost a year. She had fallen into what she called "the worst depression of my life" and wanted to see me as soon as possible.

"I can't believe this is happening," she told me at our appointment. "I think the abortion did something horrible to me. If only I hadn't been so stupid!"

"Why do you think you're stupid?"

"Why did I do it? Why did I let myself get pregnant with Stephen? Why did I let him get away with not using a condom?"

"You think that getting pregnant before has something to do with your difficulty conceiving now?" I asked.

"I don't know," she said. "I feel like . . . like I've ruined my life. Like I don't deserve to have a baby."

Patricia and her husband Stuart had been trying to conceive for almost a year and were on the verge of beginning the conventional round of fertility testing to find out whether there was a treatable problem for their infertility. The decision to become parents had been a big one for both of them. They had waited a full five years after getting married before deciding that they were both ready for a child. By then, both of them were settled in reasonably stable jobs and Patricia had decided to stay at a company she disliked, primarily because her employer's health plan had such good maternity benefits.

Patricia had been so convinced that she would become pregnant the first month they tried to conceive that she had planned her work schedule around her anticipated maternity leave. Now, after eleven months of trying, she felt certain that there had to be something wrong with her, something related to the abortion she had had in her early twenties. She was also convinced that Stuart—who deeply wanted children—would leave her if she could not become pregnant.

"If I had only known!" she said. "If someone had told me. I never would have had the abortion if I'd known I wouldn't be able to have another one!"

"What is it that you didn't know that you should have?" I asked her.

"I never should have been so . . . so *arrogant*. So *confident* that I could have a baby when I wanted one. I should have *known* that if I threw away one baby I would never have another one."

"Is that how it feels? That you threw away a baby?"

Patricia started sobbing. It took her a few seconds to catch her breath long enough to speak. "That's . . . what . . . exactly what I did."

I knew from both personal and professional experience that women grappling with the stress of infertility often blame themselves for all kinds of imagined failures and sins and that this way of thinking, though painful, gives them a way of gaining control over an essentially uncontrollable situation. But the more I tried to talk Patricia out of her guilt about her abortion—by reminding her of all the positive reasons that she had chosen it—the more self-blaming and despairing she seemed to become. The particular form her guilt took was an intense shame about keeping the abortion secret from her husband. If he ever found out, she reasoned, he would leave her.

At that point we reached an impasse in our work together. Patricia kept coming to her sessions, but she was often late and although she seemed anxious and on the verge of tears, she seemed less and less willing to talk about what was troubling her. Suspecting that she was continuing to berate herself for her previous pregnancy and abortion, I encouraged her to reveal her secret to her husband because I thought it was likely he would accept her past decision easily, and that this would help to alleviate her guilt. But she resisted these suggestions and seemed less and less motivated to talk about what was really going on for her. Things were "fine," she assured me each week, except for her inability to get pregnant. "And all the therapy in the world isn't going to help me with that!" she told me.

After a particularly difficult session in which I kept probing and she kept resisting me, it finally occurred to me that I was not hearing what she was trying to say. What kept coming up in session after session was her guilt and regret over the abortion she had had six years before. Probably because of my own commitment to the legal right to abortion, I considered early-first-trimester abortion a fairly straightforward medical procedure with few, if any, long-lasting effects. Women, I believed, should be legally entitled to choose to terminate a pregnancy they are either unwilling or unable to bring to term. But my political convictions led me to view Patricia's abortion only in the context of her empowerment. I had failed to recognize that in her present circumstances the abortion felt to her like a huge, irrevocable mistake. It was threatening to my political convictions to allow her to fully explore the range of her feelings about abortion. After all, if there was a shadow side to abortion, wouldn't those opposed to it cite the painful emotional fallout from abortions as another reason why women should not be entitled to a choice in the matter of whether to bring their pregnancies to term? Once I realized that I had been minimizing the psychological impact Patricia's abortion had on her, I began to make a concerted effort to help her express the profound regret she felt over her abortion, particularly in light of her current struggle to become pregnant again.

"If only I could go back and do it over again," Patricia told me.

"What would you have done differently?" I asked her.

"I would have *had* that baby. It would have been seven. Stuart and I would have a child to raise together. Even if it wasn't his. He would have loved it as he own, I know he would have. And if I couldn't get pregnant again, well that would have been okay. At least we would have had *that* one."

I restrained myself from pointing out the somewhat unlikely nature of this scenario and tried to stay with her instead. "What a lot of regret you have about not having that child," I remarked.

"Yes," she said, her eyes filling with tears. "I feel like I'll never be able to get over it."

"I know," I said. "But I think you will. You've got a lot of grief to get through now."

"I just never thought of it as a baby before," she said. "It was just a fetus. A clump of tissue. Nothing. But now I feel like I'm finally facing the fact that it was at least a potential life I cut off and I just feel so sorry about that."

"I know you do," I said. "I know."

In the weeks that followed, I asked Patricia to tell me in detail about how she had made the decision to have the abortion and what the actual experience had been like for her. It seemed critical that she have the opportunity to describe the experience and in some ways to both relive and reintegrate the trauma of it. She had never, she told me, discussed the abortion with anyone besides Stephen and myself, and after leaving Stephen she had tried hard to block the whole incident from her mind. It was my feeling that, like Matthew,* whose full reaction to his first son's stillbirth had been delayed for ten years until his daughter was safely delivered, Patricia also had been unable to fully process her pregnancy-abortion experience. I suspected this was due to her shame about having had an abortion (in her mind, "good girls" didn't do such things), and also to her discomfort at facing up to the intensity of her reactions to it.

The counselor she had spoken with prior to scheduling her abortion had tried to reassure her about it by telling her that at seven weeks' gestation the fetus was an unrecognizable blob of tissue and that the vacuum aspiration procedure they were going to use was very easy, relatively painless and quite safe. Rather than putting her at ease, this advice had had the unintended effect of making Patricia feel as though she was exaggerating her response to a very simple and common medical procedure. It had also

---

* Matthew's experience with stillbirth is examined in detail in Chapter Three.

served to convince her that there must be something wrong with her for being so uneasy about the procedure.

"I thought I would always have mixed feelings about it. But I also felt like I was being a big baby about the whole thing and that other women had done what they needed to do with a whole lot less fuss than I had," Patricia told me. "I tried to be as cooperative and quiet as I could during the procedure, even though it hurt… a lot! I felt like I didn't have the right to complain. I thought being a 'good' patient was a way of making up for having the abortion in the first place."

The vast majority of abortions in the United States every year take place in the first trimester. More than half occur in the first eight weeks, and 96 percent in the first fifteen weeks.[4] Because it is safer and less painful than a D&C, vacuum aspiration (in which the cervix is dilated and a tube attached to a suction machine is inserted into the uterus) has been the preferred method for first-trimester abortions since its introduction in the late 1960s.

"I still remember the horrible sound of the aspirator," Patricia told me. "It was totally unnerving."

At this time in treatment, Patricia brought in a poem she had found. An English major, Patricia had an extensive collection of poetry and literature at home, but said she'd had trouble finding any explicit references to abortion, even among female writers. After a long search, she had found what she was looking for and she wanted to read the poem out loud to me because it had affected her so deeply.

THE ABORTION

Somebody who should have been born
is gone.

Just as the earth puckered its mouth,
each bud puffing out from its knot,

I changed my shoes, and then drove south.

Up past the Blue Mountains, where
Pennsylvania humps on endlessly,
wearing, like a crayoned cat, its green hair,

its roads sunken in like a gray washboard;
where, in truth, the ground cracks evilly,
a dark socket from which the coal has poured,

*Somebody who should have been born
is gone.*

the grass as bristly and stout as chives,
and me wondering when the ground would break,
and me wondering how anything fragile survives;

up in Pennsylvania, I met a little man,
not Rumplestilskin at all, at all . . .
he took the fullness that love began.

Returning north, even the sky grew thin
like a high window looking nowhere.
The road was as flat as a sheet of tin.

*Somebody who should have been born
is gone.*

Yes, woman, such logic will lead
to loss without death. Or say what you meant,
you coward . . . this baby that I bleed.[5]

"Loss without death," I repeated. Patricia met my eyes and nod-
ded. "Like the loss that will never end?"
"Yes," she said.
Patricia's depression lifted somewhat in the months that fol-

lowed. She and her husband went through extensive fertility testing and discovered that there was a male factor in their infertility which was probably preventing them from conceiving. This was a huge relief to Patricia, and she ended up telling her husband the whole story of her previous pregnancy and abortion. In our final session together, Patricia and her husband were about to try an experimental in vitro fertilization procedure that they hoped would allow them to have the baby they wanted so much. But Patricia seemed less desperate to conceive than she had been when she had first come back into treatment with me, and she was clearly experiencing much less anguish.

"I'll be satisfied with whatever happens," she said about the outcome of the upcoming procedure. "If it works, great! If it doesn't at least we'll know we did everything that was within our power."

I was amazed by the change in Patricia's perspective. It certainly helped that she no longer felt completely responsible for the difficulties she was experiencing trying to conceive again. But it also seemed important that she had finally been able to remember and to talk about the details of her previous pregnancy and abortion. And I was able to facilitate this process once my own political convictions stopped preventing me from empathizing with her struggles to forgive herself for what had happened. She had made real progress, it seemed to me, in being able to separate her current difficulty getting pregnant from her past decision to end a pregnancy, to face up to the decision she had made and to regard her previous decision with compassion and forgiveness, *no matter what* happened in the future. I knew this wouldn't be the end of her struggles over motherhood, but I could see she had overcome one very large hurdle. She had found a way to accept responsibility for her decision, to forgive herself, and to mourn her loss.

Candace's experience with abortion was very different from Patricia's, but it bears some interesting similarities to it as well. I first interviewed Candace six months after an abortion she had after prenatal diagnostic testing revealed genetic abnormalities in the baby she was carrying. At the time of the interview she was extremely distraught and very eager to get pregnant again even though her husband was reluctant to try for another child.

The mother of two children, Candace had decided on an abortion after the results of her amniocentesis revealed that the baby had Down's syndrome. Now she was nearly beside herself with guilt for "causing so much unhappiness all around."

A large woman whose amply padded body seemed made to give comfort to others, she sat on the couch of my office pulling Kleenex after Kleenex out of the box and dabbing at her red-rimmed eyes as she spoke.

"I haven't really told anyone about what actually happened to the baby," she said. "I just couldn't. And it's just been all that much worse to get sympathy from people about losing the baby. I can't stand it! I want to tell them to shut up!"

"You told people you had a stillbirth?" I asked.

"I told them I lost the baby. And they looked so horrified and when they tried to hug me I wanted to pull away. I don't *deserve* their sympathy."

"Whose sympathy don't you think you deserve?"

"Anyone's! My mother's. I feel like I caused her so much pain. She was looking forward to another grandchild and *I'm* the only likely prospect for that! And my husband too. I don't feel like I deserve his support either. He left the decision up to me. He said he would support me either way. But it was all just so awful. The whole thing. And he's really depressed now and I feel like I made the wrong decision."

Candace and her husband Larry had received the news that their baby had a chromosomal abnormality called trisomy 21 (otherwise known as Down syndrome) several weeks following an amniocentesis which her doctor had strongly advised her to take, given the fact that she was forty-one when she became pregnant and thus ran a one in forty-eight[6] risk that her baby would have a chromosomal abnormality of some kind. Although she had not liked the idea of doing anything to interfere with her pregnancy, Candace had agreed to the test, which involves extracting a small amount of amniotic fluid through an ultrasound-guided needle injected through the uterine wall. She did not find the procedure itself particularly painful, but on the way to the hospital she had felt quite ill from the stress of it all—just the idea of the needle going into her uterus. What if they slipped? What if they hurt the baby? After they withdrew the needle they showed her on the ultrasound screen that her baby's heart was continuing to beat strongly, just as it had before the test, and she was greatly relieved.

Although the pregnancy had been an unintentional one—the apparent result of a diaphragm failure—it had not been an unwelcome turn of events, at least for Candace. At the time she discovered she was pregnant, the couple's two other children, aged eight and ten, were becoming less dependent on her for constant physical and emotional caretaking. A stay-at-home mother, Candace was the epitome of devotion, unlike the mother who had raised her.

Candace's mother was a heavy drinker who was subject to fits of rage when she drank. She often hit, slapped and shook her children in anger. The youngest of five children, Candace said she had always felt, growing up, that there was "not enough of anything to go around—not enough money, enough food, enough love." As a result, she said, she "grew up feeling hungry, especially for love."

When she started a family of her own, Candace made a conscious vow to provide for her own children what she never had as a child—a steady, emotionally supportive presence and plenty of everything. For the most part, she had succeeded very well in this regard. Her two boys were healthy and confident and appeared to be thriving. But they were growing up and needing her less. Though she and Larry had decided, after their second baby was born, not to have any more children—mostly because of financial strain—when she discovered she was pregnant, Candace was actually more pleased than distressed. The idea of another baby to nurture was tremendously appealing to her.

Her husband, though, was still afraid of the additional financial burden of another child, and he didn't relish the thought of taking on another period of intensive caretaking for a baby just when the boys were finally becoming a great deal more independent. Larry raised the idea of an abortion in the first trimester, but he met with such vehement disapproval from Candace that he quickly resigned himself to having a third child. The amniocentesis results, however, sent both Larry and Candace into a tailspin.

Their baby girl had Down syndrome, which causes varying degrees of mental retardation and sometimes other birth defects such as heart problems. There was no way of predicting the degree of mental or physical impairment, but she would almost certainly be born with the distinctive facial features of those affected by the chromosomal abnormality: a flat face, slanting eyes, and low-set ears.[7]

"You never think it's going to happen to you," Candace said. "I knew I was in a higher risk category because of my age but the odds were still really low. I really didn't imagine that it would happen to me. I was shocked. But I knew I couldn't handle a baby like that. The doctor didn't know how bad off the baby would be; she might have been pretty functional or she might have been in terrible shape with no hope of improvement. I imagined the worst—all I could imagine was a little girl with blank eyes not understanding anything that was going on around her. I knew we couldn't handle it. I mean if I hadn't known about it ahead of time I would have just coped. But if I had a choice, I'd rather not. I know that sounds terrible, but it's true. I remember when they called me to say there was a problem, they had already scheduled the abortion for the next day. I was relieved it was all set up. We had an appointment to see the doctor and the genetics counselor the next morning and then in the afternoon . . . I had . . . the . . . procedure." Candace reached for another Kleenex and blew her nose.

"It's still very fresh in your mind," I remarked.

"Yeah," she said. "But it's unreal too. Like a nightmare."

Candace had a medical induction at twenty-four weeks into her pregnancy. Only one-half of 1 percent of abortions take place after fifteen weeks of pregnancy each year, however, and one of the most commonly used procedures in the late second trimester is medical induction, in which the physician injects a saline solution into the uterus which induces contractions and dilates the cervix to assist in expulsion of the baby. The procedure alters intracellular pressure in the uterus, and any fetal movement usually ceases within one hour after the injection. Contractions generally begin within twelve to twenty-four hours after the saline solution is injected, and delivery occurs six to eight hours later. These contractions are painful: the mother may receive analgesic medication but is conscious during the procedure and during labor and delivery. The most common method of abortion used earlier in the second trimester is dilatation and evacuation (D&E), which *is* performed under either local or general anesthesia and is similar to vacuum aspiration but requires a greater dilation of the cervix and may, depending on the size of the fetus, require the use of forceps and dismemberment of the fetus (depending on its size) in addition to the suction machine.[8] Candace was given a choice between a D&E and an induction and she had opted for the latter, although she knew that the labor and delivery would be grueling.

"I was tempted to ask them to do the D&E and just put me under for the whole thing," Candace told me. "But I didn't think that was really right. It was my baby and I thought I should deliver her if I could."

Candace couldn't bring herself to discuss the details of her induction during the first interview I had with her. When we spoke again, almost a year later, she told me the doctor and several of the attending nurses were distinctly unsympathetic to the pain she was in.

"I wish I hadn't done it. I wish someone had told me how bad I'd feel afterwards if I did it!" she cried. "I see these protesters at the abortion clinics on TV trying to block women from going inside and I think—this is awful I know—but I think to myself I wish somebody had stopped me! I mean I know I had a right to do what I did, I know it was *my* choice, but still . . ."

In the months following the abortion Candace's husband Larry became increasingly withdrawn. She interpreted his retreat as an indication that he both regretted the abortion and blamed her for the decision. His reluctance to participate in trying to conceive another baby seemed like proof to her that he was trying to punish her.

"I feel like having another baby is the only way to make things okay again," Candace told me at the end of our first interview. "And I don't think I'm ever going to be able to."

After she left my office I thought about how important it was to Candace to be a good mother to her children, and how much of her identity depended on that role. At the time there was a great deal of controversy about a proposed congressional bill banning so-called partial birth abortions (also known as intact D&E's). Proponents of the ban were calling the procedure inhumane and unnecessary. Even though Candace had not had this particular procedure, I felt certain that the implied condemnation of all those who have late-term abortions had affected her. I wondered whether part of her struggle with her decision to end her third pregnancy was centered on what appeared to be a fundamental contradiction between her image of herself as a good mother and the fact that she had had a late-term abortion.

The next time I saw Candace was more than a year and a half

after her abortion. I was surprised to see how different she looked since we had last met. Her long hair, which she had pulled severely back from her face in a simple ponytail, had been cut into a short and flattering hairstyle. Her eyes were brighter, much less dulled by the pain she had been in the last time I'd seen her. I remarked on how well she looked.

"I'm taking much better care of myself," she told me. "I feel better. It must be true what they say about it just takes time to heal."

"Is that all that's happened? Time has passed?" I asked skeptically. The change in both her mood and her appearance was so dramatic that I wondered whether some major shift had taken place in her life. Had she finally succeeded in becoming pregnant, perhaps?

"Oh no," she said, laughing, as if reading my mind. "I'm not pregnant, if that's what you're thinking! Actually Larry and I have decided not to try for any more kids. I'm going back to get my master's degree in the fall, so there really wouldn't be the time! And it's okay . . . I'm more at peace with myself. More accepting of what happened."

As we spoke it became clear to me that a number of significant things had happened to make such a striking difference in Candace's attitude. For one thing, she and her husband had been fortunate enough to meet another couple who had experienced genetic abortions at a support group meeting for neonatal loss.

"I was afraid to go to the meeting the first night," Candace told me. "I thought I would be the only one there who had had an abortion. I wasn't sure I would be able to tell them the truth about how I had lost the baby. But thank God there was another couple there who had been through the same thing and they were the nicest people. Everyone felt just as sorry for what they had been through as they did for the women who'd had stillbirths. That made a big impression on me. I guess I had a weird idea about what anyone who had a genetic abortion would be like. I felt like a cold, selfish person for having one . . . I guess I thought anyone else who had one would be . . . kind of . . . I don't know . . . self-centered, uncaring. But this one couple, they were really just nice, intelligent, caring people who had been through a rough time and were trying to do the best they knew how for themselves and their family. I admired the courage it took for them to speak up at those meetings and then I started to feel like maybe I wasn't such an awful person either and that even though we had *chosen* our loss we still really grieved for our baby . . . we grieved just like all the other people in the support group. And I started to realize that this other couple and us had been thrown into a situation that was kind of like the one in that movie, you know . . . *Sophie's Choice*? You know that scene, it's what everything is based on, the scene where she's told by the Nazis that she can only save one of her children but she has to choose which one? She has to choose which one will live and which one will die. And at first she says, 'NO! I can't choose!' and they tell her if she doesn't she'll lose both of them. So finally she pushes her daughter towards the guard and he takes her hand and walks her off to the gas chamber. And Sophie feels so guilty about it for the rest of her life that she can't live with herself, and that's why she gets involved with this crazy man who punishes her all the time, because she hates herself so much."

"Yes," I said. "I do remember that movie. But it sounds to me like there's a difference between you and Sophie."

She gave me a puzzled look and I continued.

"You've found a way to live with your choice and Sophie didn't."

Candace thought about this for a moment and then she said, "Maybe. At least I think I'm beginning to get there. I didn't want to lose that baby. She was a wanted child. But I know if I'd had her we'd all have suffered a lot. And what would have happened to her when Larry and I died? I couldn't bear the idea of her rotting away in an institution somewhere, with no one to visit her. I still feel real sad about this, I probably always will. But I know something now that maybe I didn't know before. The reason I made that decision, that choice, was not because I wanted to cause more suffering and pain. The reason I made it was because I was trying to relieve the suffering for everyone: Larry and the kids, and even me. Maybe I was wrong. Maybe I could have handled it. Maybe we could have handled it. Maybe, and I hate to think about it this way, but maybe we all could have *benefited* by the experience. But I had to decide and that's what I did, good or bad, right or wrong."

"It sounds to me like you're a very good mother," I remarked.

"I hope I am. I try to be . . . I think . . . what I really believe is that every child has a right to be born into a home where they're wanted and where the mother (and hopefully the father too!) is ready and willing to be there for them while they're growing up. It's a huge responsibility to be a good parent and you need to take that responsibility seriously. I hope that's what I did. That's what I tried to do."

If there is little common understanding of the plight of those who must decide whether to continue a pregnancy in the face of fetal abnormalities, there is probably even less appreciation for the dilemma faced by those who, often after using fertility drugs or assisted reproductive technology, discover they have a multiple pregnancy—twins, triplets, quadruplets or even quintuplets—and must decide whether to reduce their number by aborting one or more of the fetuses. Fetal risks of multiple gestation include increased rates of miscarriage, birth defects and premature delivery—along with the mental and physical problems that can accompany a premature birth.[9] Maternal risks of multiple gestation include pregnancy-induced high blood pressure or preeclampsia, diabetes, and premature labor and delivery. Multifetal

pregnancy reductions are performed in the hospital on an outpa-
tient basis, and involve inserting a needle, guided by ultrasound,
through either the woman's abdomen or her vagina. The needle is
used to inject potassium chloride into a fetus, halting its development. Ironically, many of those facing a decision about multifetal
pregnancy reduction have spent a significant amount of time,
money and energy trying to conceive.

This is the situation Sue and her husband Allan found themselves in after having struggled with unexplained infertility for
nearly seven years, prior to conceiving their first child through
IVF. When they started trying for their second child their next
two IVF cycles resulted in pregnancies (of single babies), both of
which ended in devastating miscarriages. After the next IVF
attempt they were surprised to find Sue was pregnant with
quadruplets, or possibly quintuplets.

"It all happened so quickly," Sue told me during our interview
in her home. I could hear the voices of young children rising, peri-
odically, in the background. "It was kind of like at the time we
found out about the multiple pregnancy I really didn't feel like I
had a whole lot of choice about reducing it. And I was pretty
much told by the doctors, 'Oh, well, you're not going to *carry* that
many babies.' And most likely it would have to be reduced to two.
And not knowing anything about it, we thought that was just the
way it was. Then my husband just happened to mention at a con-
sultation that if we could keep all four babies we would, and that's
the first time anyone mentioned the possibility of keeping three.
We went through a very difficult decision-making process at that
time, and then on the day of the reduction it was really, really hard.
But afterwards, I just focused back on the pregnancy, and I was
concentrating on the birth of the triplets. So, the loss of the one
was pretty far on the back burner for awhile."

"So you had kind of a delayed reaction to it?" I asked.

"Yes, I think I did. My triplets are two and a half now. After they were born, I started reading *The Triplet Connection* magazine. There were all these stories people wrote about how glad they were that they had kept all their babies—even quadruplets and quintuplets—so my feelings about [the reduction] started coming up again. I had such a good pregnancy with the triplets, that it's hard not to wonder whether that fourth one might have been okay too."

"So there were only four after all?"

"The fifth one never developed. So that wasn't an issue. But after the triplets were born, every three months, when I would get the magazine, my feelings about the reduction would come up again. And each time I would have to go over the whole decision-making process that my husband and I went through, and come to terms again with why we did what we did. Then I would feel pretty resolved about it. It would always come down to the fact that we did the best we could with the information we had at the time, and the triplets we have may have been so healthy and the pregnancy may have been so good because it was three and not four. And the bottom line is we won't ever really know."

"Yeah, that uncertainty must be hard to live with. How are things going for you now?"

"Well, intellectually I know all the reasons we made that decision, but emotionally there's still an ache that will probably always be there, especially when I hear about quads . . . but not on an everyday basis . . . For the most part I feel I'm as settled as I'm going to be with it. But there is an ache that comes up."

"I'm sure there is."

"There was a lot of loss in that period of time just before the triplets came along and all of the losses got kind of clumped together. I'd had two miscarriages that had happened spontaneously. And I lost my sister at that time too, and my doctor was really good about talking to me about all of that before we tried the next [IVF] procedure, making sure we felt able to cope with another try, after all these losses. There was a lot of loss but the blessing was the triplets, that they all came to be."

"That must have helped."

"It did. I felt like I had the three all at once instead of just one because two of the babies I lost through miscarriage were kind of coming back to me. I lost the baby during the reduction too but I've since had a fifth child—without our even doing IVF or any-thing—so I feel like all the babies I lost, came back to me one way or another."

"Yes. I see what you mean. Do you think about the babies you lost a lot?"

"Not every day. But spiritually, and emotionally, it's there for me. Thinking about them coming back to me in this way is one of my ways of coping with it."

"Was the reduction different, I mean emotionally, from the mis-carriages?"

"In many ways, it was. Because we had to choose. We had felt so little control over things when we were struggling with infer-tility and then suddenly we had this choice to make, this control and we didn't like it at all. We had been trying for so many years to create life, it was very contradictory and painful to have to make that decision."

"It sounds like it. Did you feel like you got enough emotional support during the pregnancy reduction?"

"No, not really. Mostly because the people we talked to mainly were doctors and medical people and they were all coming from the point of view that it was dangerous medically to carry that many babies—and I think from that point of view they're proba-bly right . . . but because that was the only side I was getting, I wished later that I'd known I had more of choice to keep all four. I might still have made the same decision, I really don't know, but I felt like there was a whole emotional piece missing . . . and also no one ever said we could *consider* keeping all four and I think now, why wasn't that an option?"

"It must be hard to look back at that aspect of it."

"It is, although I'm not blaming anyone; I just wish I'd had another point of view to consider."

"Yes. So you felt unsupported in that way."

"Right. And another reason we lost a lot of emotional support is because we didn't tell very many people about the reduction. We made that decision because we felt like our family members wouldn't understand it—just the whole Catholic thing. We decided that the last thing we needed was to have people around us who were saying they were supportive but we knew they really weren't. We only told a very few people. That way we had more control over how we dealt with it without all these other opinions to deal with, but the downside was that we had almost no one to talk to about it . . . in the long run that doesn't always feel so great."

"When in the pregnancy did they do the reduction? Towards the end of the first trimester?"

"Yes. Our doctors told us that the pregnancy might reduce on its own to three by that time; that happens. But ours was still quadruplets. And we didn't know what the genders of the babies were."

"And did you—I know this might be a difficult question to answer—but how did you decide which one to reduce? Did you leave it up to the doctor?"

"Yes. They really just . . . picked the smallest baby," she said, her voice choking, beginning to cry. "I'm really feeling the loss now, because . . . that little one . . . just because it was little, you know . . . lost its life."

"It must have been such a hard thing to go through."

"Yes, it was . . . we had to make a decision, and neither one of us wanted to make that decision . . . we don't want to think about that fourth one, you know. Because we have five kids now, the oldest is five years old . . . and I feel very blessed for the five that we have but I think that, for the three that I lost, I'll always have an ache for them. And I'll always think about them because I feel like, that's all they're going to have. And if I don't say a prayer for them, then nobody will."

"Yes. I think you've found a nice way to honor them. And a comforting way to think about things, too."

"One thing I forgot to tell you. You know I lost my sister right around the same time as the multiple pregnancy and . . . I do feel like she needed some babies to hold too. . . . My sister knew about the two miscarriages, but she didn't know about the triplets. But I feel like in a way, she's taking care of my lost babies until . . . until whenever."

For Patricia, Candace, and Sue, the fact that their pregnancy losses were chosen did not make their grief over them any less real or less potent. In many respects, the fact that the loss was "chosen" made it more complicated and problematic to resolve. And the censorship imposed by both sides of the current political debate only made it harder.

This is true for many women. There are certainly those for whom an abortion is experienced as a tremendous relief from an untenable situation; these tend to be women who are quite confident about their choice, and who, for whatever reason, have few if any regrets about it. But for others, the decision to terminate a pregnancy represents a moral dilemma which must be resolved before the matter is settled emotionally. Part of that resolution involves accepting responsibility for the decision, owning the loss, and finding a way to forgive oneself.

Unfortunately in today's politically polarized climate there are very few resources available to assist women in this important process. Consequently, many women carry around unresolved feelings of guilt and shame which can tend to get expressed in self-punishing thoughts and behavior. Finding a place to remember and talk about one's abortion experience—in support groups, in psychotherapy, or among friends—and demonstrating one's caring through rituals or ceremonies which honor the aborted beings can help in the process of reconciling one's view of oneself as a good person with the fact of having terminating a pregnancy.

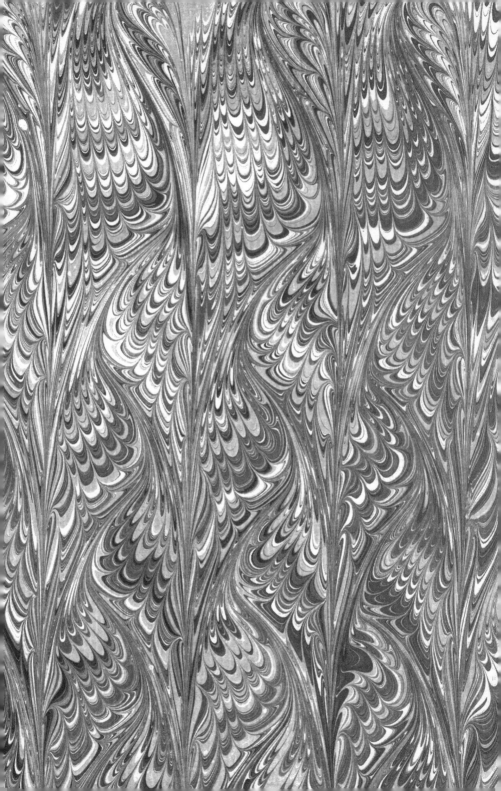

Lost Fathers: Men's Experience of Pregnancy Loss and Abortion

> *. . . And it's come to this,*
> *A man can't speak of his own child that's dead . . .*
> . . . .
> *. . . I'm not so much*
> *Unlike other folks*
> *as your standing there*
> *Apart would make me out . . .*
> —ROBERT FROST[1]

HEN I WAS conducting the research for this chapter I made two interesting and seemingly contradictory discoveries. The first was that it was extremely difficult to find research studies or literature on the psychological impact of pregnancy loss and abortion on men. Although fairly extensive literature on the psychological impact of pregnancy loss and, especially, abortion, does exist, these studies tend to focus almost exclusively on women's experiences.[2]

The other unexpected phenomenon was how easy it was to find men whose partners had experienced pregnancy losses or abortions to interview. From the lack of attention paid to men's emotional reactions to virtually any matter related to procreation, one might be tempted to conclude that such research is simply not necessary since men are obviously unaffected by these issues. However, the eagerness with which the individual men I approached seized the opportunity to speak about their experiences told an entirely different story. Though it is inaccurate to make generalizations about the attributes of either gender, my impression is that many modern men are highly invested in their wives' pregnancies yet often feel excluded from full participation in any discussion of them. As one man I spoke with put it: "Believe it or not, men have feelings too!"

It is a deeply held belief in our culture that men are only remotely affected by matters related to reproductive issues. This belief may have its origins in the biological fact that after the moment of conception, the father's role in childbearing is necessarily restricted to protecting and providing for his pregnant mate. He can only indirectly care for his unborn offspring. It is not, of course, his body which nourishes, shelters, and gives birth to the baby. It is not his abdomen that swells so visibly or increasingly restricts his activities. Only vicariously can he experience the awesome sensation of the movement of a new being, as he places his hand on his mate's belly and feels the baby's head.

Although few men will admit to feelings of deprivation about not being biologically equipped to bear children, this sense of deprivation has been acknowledged by psychoanalysts, such as Edith Jacobson, who found that the "conspicuous disinterest in having children" on the part of many of her male patients "regularly proves to be a stubborn defense against a deeply repressed envy of woman's reproductive abilities."[3] This phenomenon is also commonly observed by parents of preschool-aged boys, who are fond of parading around with pillows under their shirts announcing that they, like mommy, are going to have a baby. There appears to be a good deal more empirical evidence, in fact, for the existence of "womb envy" in boys than there is for "penis envy" in girls.

Of course in our culture, the minute a boy expresses the wish to have a baby he is strongly discouraged from such silly notions. As soon as boys reach school age, they are quickly indoctrinated into their gender roles by the vehement teasing of peers and older boys should they express any interest in such girlish activities as "playing mommy"—which naturally includes having and caring for babies.

Certainly, it is a necessary part of a boy's psychological separation from his mother to begin to identify with males rather than with females at a certain point in his development, but the degree to which very young boys seem to feel compelled to disown all feminine activities makes them much more limited in their activities, at an earlier age, than girls are today. The growing social awareness that females need not be restricted to nurturant, supportive roles in life has given rise to more female participation in the workplace and on the athletic field, but boys have not been similarly applauded for cultivating an interest in domesticity, or any type of nurturing or cooperative activity. Young girls are still playing with dolls, but they are joining soccer teams in droves. Young boys are by and large still doing what they were a generation ago: competing in athletics.

Although many two-career households have moved toward less rigid male and female roles with regard to childbearing and raising—more men are seen with infants and children in tow, and certainly many more are actively participating in the delivery of their children—men seem to be participating in these traditionally female responsibilities in addition to fulfilling the traditional male role of providing for and protecting the family. Although they may share the breadwinning role with their wives, men still seem to feel primarily responsible for keeping the family afloat financially.

Despite the fact that they may receive gratitude and appreciation from the women in their lives for taking on more responsibilities in caring for their young, very few men receive a positive response from their bosses and colleagues for such behavior. In fact, quite the opposite is often the case: many men are ridiculed, punished or viewed as unprofessional for taking time away from work to care for their children, just as they were ridiculed for playing with dolls when they were younger. As a result, men tend to feel conflicted about their household responsibilities and are embarrassed to admit the extent of their involvement with child-rearing, as if such interest disqualified them from bona fide participation in the world of serious work.

And so it remains as true today as it was a generation ago that boys, in learning to identify with members of their own gender, find it necessary to repress their natural sense of wonder regarding procreation and, along with it, any disappointment they may feel in not being able to bear children themselves. The long-held assumptions that men don't bond with their children until after birth, that they are overwhelmed by anything related to pregnancy and childbirth, and that they are incapable of the same degree of connection with their children as women continue more or less unchallenged.

In my professional experience, however, I have found time and time again that men are actually quite involved in the pregnancies they help to create, even though they may be inhibited about openly expressing the depth of that involvement. They are afraid that this will make them appear "unmanly," and they have often received rather clear messages from the women in their lives that they are intruding on female territory by claiming such a strong connection.

In a study conducted in 1976 among men participating in childbirth preparation classes,[4] it was found that 75 percent felt they shared in their wives' pregnancy to such a large degree that they felt the pregnancy was happening to both themselves and their wives.

However, when the wives were asked whether they thought that their husbands shared their pregnancies in this way, a majority of them answered "no."[5] My guess is that not many more would answer yes today.

Part of the reason may be that women, not having gained full entry into the traditionally male domain of work, have been reluctant to wholeheartedly admit men into the female realm of childbearing or to share significantly their decision-making power in that arena. One of the complaints I hear most frequently from women in couples therapy is that their husbands, though sharing the burden of caring for babies and young children, are not "doing it right"—which, they claim, forces them to do it themselves. Certainly there are cases in which a man acts out his conflicts about participation in childrearing activities by passive-aggressively neglecting certain key responsibilities, but in many cases I have observed it is more a matter of the woman's jealously guarding her power in the home that is the problem.

Whether it is conscious or not, women's insistence on absolute authority in matters related to procreation and childrearing, and their view of their husbands as incapable of the same level of care and involvement as they are, leave men with little incentive to take on a more active role in that arena. In fact, quite the reverse is true: men who are excluded from important decisions related to their children, or who are ridiculed for their domestic incompetence, learn to view themselves as hopelessly inept and eventually become even less involved as nurturant parents. It is truly a self-fulfilling prophecy.

Neglecting to consider the profound impact of creating a new life on men gives them the message that they ought not to be involved. It is as if there were a huge KEEP OUT sign on the door to the women's room. This leaves men who are earnestly seeking a deeper level of involvement with their children completely shut out.

It is this exclusion that Robert Frost protests in his 1914 poem

"Home Burial," from which the epigraph to this chapter is taken. The following excerpts describe a couple's struggle to comprehend each other's reactions to the death of their firstborn child:

> He saw her from the bottom of the stairs
> Before she saw him. She was starting down,
> Looking back over her shoulder at some fear.
> She took a doubtful step and then undid it
> To raise herself and look again. He spoke
> Advancing toward her: "What is it you see
> From up there always—for I want to know."
> She turned and sank upon her skirts at that,
> And her face changed from terrified to dull.
> He said to gain time: "What is it you see,"
> Mounting until she cowered under him.
> "I will find out now—you must tell me, dear."
> She, in her place, refused him any help
> With the least stiffening of her neck and silence.
> She let him look, sure that he wouldn't see,
> Blind creature; and awhile he didn't see.
> But at last he murmured, "Oh," and again, "Oh."
>
> "What is it—what?" she said.
>   "Just that I see.
>
> . . . .
> But I understand: it is not the stones,
> But the child's mound—
>
> . . . .
> Let me into your grief. I'm not so much
> Unlike other folks as your standing there
> Apart would make me out. Give me my chance. . . ."[6]

For men who are deeply connected to the pregnancies of their mates, the "psychic gestation" that takes place tends to parallel the baby's growth. In the first trimester, when there are few tangible signs of the pregnancy's reality apart from the positive pregnancy test and his mate's tiredness and nausea, a man may have a sense of disbelief about his impending fatherhood. As one man puts it:

> *I knew my wife was pregnant. I'd even been with her when she took the home pregnancy test. I saw the color change. And I was with her when the doctor's office called with the news that the pregnancy test was positive. I had conclusive evidence but nothing had really changed much. She didn't look any different. She didn't act very different either. It was hard to believe that there was actually a baby coming.*

But when tangible proof of the fetus's existence is obtained— either by seeing images of the baby on the ultrasound screen or by hearing its heartbeat or by noticing the thickening of his mate's waist—a man's reactions to becoming a father are likely to become more conscious:

> *When I saw the shadow of the baby's body on the ultrasound screen . . . that's when I finally realized we were really going to have a baby. It all came crashing in on me at once: I was going to be a father!*

Many men have strong feelings of identification with their pregnant mates and may even develop physical symptoms which echo the pregnancy. On the other hand, as Libby and Arthur Coleman point out in their book *Pregnancy: The Psychological Experience,* some men may feel defensive and may go so far as to "develop super-masculine hobbies as if to counteract the strong feminine pull that threatens to engulf them."[7]

And, of course, fathers-to-be struggle with the same unconscious fears as their mates about reenacting the childhood disappointments they experienced at their father's knee, while still entertaining the hope that they might compensate for those failures in their relationship with their own children:

> *When I realized that I was going to be a father I really got nervous. I felt like it was going to be a huge burden I wouldn't be able to handle. My own dad always seemed so tied down by family things . . . there was always the mortgage to pay and all the bills from all us kids . . . it scared me that it might happen to me too . . . and then my kid would feel guilty just like I had.*

As the Colemans point out, the "huge psychological changes of fatherhood tend to be overshadowed by the dramatic physiological changes of the woman."[8] In our culture we tend to regard fatherhood as beginning at birth rather than at conception. As a result men are not seen as being intensely affected by the pregnancy losses and abortions they are involved in, and they tend to keep whatever reactions they have to these events to themselves, in deference to their female partner's feelings.

Despite these inhibiting factors, the number of first-person accounts of men's experiences with infertility and pregnancy loss in the popular media has been increasing.[9] Still, on the whole the topic of men's emotional responses to reproductive failures of all kinds, and especially their reactions to abortions they are party to, remains shrouded in almost complete silence. It is entirely possible that this silence and sense of exclusion from the decision-making process regarding abortions has contributed to the vehemence with which some men seem to be desperate to reassert control over women's pregnancies (attempting to force them, in the most extreme cases, to bear every child they conceive, even in cases of rape and incest). This silence can also tremendously complicate the resolution of men's feelings about the pregnancy losses they are

involved in, and thus can interfere with their ability to successful-
ly adapt to later pregnancies, aggravate their relationships with the
women in their lives, and profoundly, if unconsciously, affect their
feelings about themselves as fathers.

This was true of Carl, a twenty-eight-year-old man I saw in my
practice, whose unresolved feelings about an abortion he had been
party to with his live-in girlfriend years before had a profound but
completely unconscious impact on his reaction to his current
wife's pregnancy and subsequent miscarriage. Carl was referred to
me by a colleague who was treating Carl and his wife in couples'
therapy. The couples' therapist had advised each of them to under-
take individual psychotherapy in addition to the couples' work
because he felt that a number of unexplored individual issues (on
both sides) were causing a stalemate that threatened the very
integrity of the marriage.

In the initial brief conversation I had with him on the phone,
Carl indicated to me that he was not at all convinced that he
"needed therapy," but that he felt under pressure to "do something" since his wife was threatening to leave him, and he was not
prepared to "let her go." As psychotherapy under duress is rarely
productive, I suggested that we meet for a single session to assess
the situation so that he could decide whether or not psychotherapy would be helpful to him. He seemed relieved to be given the
authority to decide for himself whether he wanted to be in treatment. At our first meeting, he talked a great deal about how
demanding his wife was and how frustrating it was to him that,
according to her, nothing he did was ever "enough." He said he
had almost gotten to the point where he ceased to care whether
she followed through on her increasing threats to leave him. When
I asked him what kinds of things his wife complained about, he
said, "Everything. I work too much. I'm too worried about money.
I won't talk to her. I don't want to try to have a kid."

This last issue, Carl told me, was the key area of disagreement between them. About a year and a half prior to that time Carl's wife had become pregnant. This was shortly after their marriage, and only four months after they had met. Their attraction to one another had been intense, and because Carl's wife tended toward impulsivity (while Carl himself tended to be rather passive) they had married in a matter of months. Carl had reluctantly agreed that his new wife should stop taking her birth control pills when they married—the possibility of a pregnancy added a lot of excitement to their lovemaking—but Carl himself was secretly relieved when, for the first couple of months, his wife continued to get her period as usual.

The third month of their marriage was different. He was aware that she hadn't announced the "bad news" that her period had arrived for quite some time. And when she finally did tell him she was pregnant his feelings were so conflicted that he did not celebrate the news with the same kind of enthusiasm she did. This infuriated her. "Can't you ever be happy about anything?" she had asked him sarcastically.

After that, Carl had begun to withdraw from his wife emotionally. Nearly all communication between them ceased. Then she started talking about getting an abortion, since, as she put it, "What was the point of having the damn baby anyway?" The proposal to have an abortion was horrifying to Carl. Although he was terrified by the idea of the huge responsibility of becoming a father (mostly because his own experience being fathered had been so disappointing), he was repulsed by the idea that his wife might have an abortion, and he told her so. "Well then do something!" she had pleaded with him. "You've got to help me with this! I'm not having this baby alone!" Carl told her he didn't know what she wanted from him, and several days later, in her tenth week of pregnancy, Carl's wife had a miscarriage.

While she was at home for several days after the D&C, Carl was working very long days at his business. Things suddenly got very busy at work and his presence, he said, was "absolutely critical." His wife started making snide remarks about what an "important person" he was, and Carl would just refuse to speak to her or would leave the room.

Finally, Carl told me, his wife confronted him. "I had just gotten home from work. It was a really late night, I was exhausted. She had this thing about wanting us to find out the real reason for the miscarriage, even though the doctors had already said they didn't know why it happened, only that it wasn't chromosomal, which meant it might have been due to immunological factors but it was hard to tell. Anyway, she kept pushing me to call the doctor back and get more information or set up another appointment or something and I said I would, just to get her off my back, but I have to admit I did keep putting it off because I didn't think it was going to do any good. And so when I walked in that night she said something like if I didn't call the doctor the next day she was never going to believe anything I said again and I got so damned angry . . . I'd just had it! So I said . . . well I said something to her like, 'What difference does it make to *you? You're* the one who was ready to throw the baby in the trash,' . . . and she . . . well I wish I hadn't said that afterwards. It really hurt her."

Since the miscarriage, Carl's wife had been very eager to become pregnant again and Carl had been somewhat uncooperative. Although he had agreed to start trying to conceive a few months after the miscarriage, business trips frequently kept him away from home during his wife's most fertile days. He said his wife was "fed up with his excuses" and was threatening to move out if he was not willing to make their relationship and having a baby more of a priority.

"Well it sounds like you're really stuck," I observed. "On the one hand, you don't want her to leave, but on the other hand you're not so sure you want to become a father either."

"That's right," he answered. "I can't win."

"Win?" I asked.

"Well, yeah. Either she wins and we have a baby or I win and we don't."

At the end of that first session I asked Carl whether he wanted to continue coming to therapy to explore some possible solutions to the dilemma he was in with his wife. He thought that would "be a good idea," but he reserved the right to reassess whether he wanted to keep coming to therapy after eight more sessions together. I could see that having more authority in relation to both me and his own psychotherapy than he seemed to have in his relationship to his wife was critically important to Carl. I felt that at least part of the difficulty he was experiencing in his relationship with his wife was that he was somewhat intimidated by her and that he tended to assert himself only passively and indirectly (such as by not being available during her ovulation). This only contributed to the problems between them because it left both of them feeling frustrated and unclear about what was going on. Since the therapeutic environment is a place where patients often can try out and practice some new behaviors that can be useful when transferred to the rest of their lives, I strongly endorsed his proposal to keep the therapy time-limited. I also emphasized the fact that he was the one with the authority to decide whether to continue treatment or not.

"I like that idea," I told him. "And I think it might be useful for us to explore what it is about fatherhood that is unattractive to you."

"All right," he said. "I'll think about it."

In the next several months we uncovered a great deal in Carl's past that seemed related to his uneasiness about becoming a father. His own father had been a work-obsessed but only modestly successful salesman. He had worked for a number of different companies but he never seemed to get promoted to higher levels. Larry thought this was because his father was so timid and self-effacing.

His father complained frequently about the pressures of his job and his feelings of entrapment. He even told his young son that he should wait to get married and have children until he'd had a chance to enjoy himself in life, as he never had, having been married just out of high school and having four children by the time he was twenty-five years old.

Carl had been the only boy in the family, with two older sisters and one younger. In therapy, Carl talked about his feelings of "being outnumbered" at home and wishing his father had "saved him" by taking him out to do "father-son activities like fishing or camping." But he never did, Carl said, because he was either too busy working or too tired.

"My dad always made a lot of promises he didn't keep," Carl told me, his eyes seeming to moisten a little, and his voice sounding more constricted. "He always said we were going to go fishing. He was going to take me to this special place he used to fish at when he was a boy. He kept promising and promising. Then one Christmas he asked me if I wanted a fishing rod and I said no. I was sure he wouldn't come through, so why get my hopes up? And he said to me, 'What's wrong? Don't you believe me? You don't believe I'm going to take you with me?' But he never did . . . even though he bought me the stupid fishing rod."

Carl described his mother as a strongly opinionated woman who was highly critical of his father. Larry thought his father had been dominated by his mother and that this was the source of his misery.

"Maybe," Carl said during one session, "maybe I just want to make sure that what happened to my dad doesn't happen to me."

When I asked him what he meant by this, he said, "Well my wife . . . she's . . . you know I've told you she's very . . . strong willed. She's not afraid to say what she thinks. And I admire that. Her mind works real fast too. She can outdo me every time. Just like my mom did with my dad. He'd just be standing there speechless when they had an argument. And my wife . . . well she's a lot like that. I mean she's *strong*. And maybe I'm just being so stubborn about this baby thing because, well . . . because I'm afraid I'll turn into my father and have a miserable, pathetic life like he did . . . and maybe I feel like I have to finally take a stand!"

"Take a stand?" I asked.

"Yeah . . . you know like I never have before . . . especially with women."

"Which women?"

"My mother. I could never talk back to her! There'd be hell to pay. And my girlfriend, even though I really should have with her!"

"Why?" I asked him.

"I don't know . . . we were living together for a few years and she was planning to go back to school to get her degree only she got pregnant—she was on the pill but I think she forgot to take it a few times—and I . . . well she just told me she'd take care of it which meant she'd get an abortion and I said 'Okay, whatever you want' and I helped her pay for it and all. But afterwards I realized she'd never even asked me how I felt about it! Like that was just completely beside the point."

"Did you feel like you might have wanted to have the baby?" I asked.

"Maybe . . . I wanted to be able . . . to at least discuss it . . . but there didn't seem to be any point in doing that. Her mind was made up."

"So you felt like she wouldn't have listened to you?"

"I know she wouldn't have," he said.

"But *you* didn't tell her how you felt either?" I asked.

"It wouldn't have made any difference," he said.

"It sounds like you still have a lot of resentment about what happened."

"You're right," he said. "I do."

Carl had never spoken to anyone about the abortion, partly out of a concern for keeping his girlfriend's secret and partly because he was so ashamed of his behavior during that time. He expressed a great deal of regret about not having "taken a stand" at the time that he learned of his girlfriend's pregnancy. He felt he had let both his child and himself down by not speaking up. He was ashamed of this and did not want to talk about it.

"You know, it seems to me that your resentments about what happened during that time might have something to do with your feelings about becoming a father now," I told him.

"How?"

"Well . . . you told me you were very angry about what happened, that it wasn't right that you didn't have a say in whether your girlfriend was going to get an abortion or not, and I wonder whether dragging your feet about trying to have another baby now is a way of 'taking the stand' you weren't able to take then."

"You mean I'm just being stubborn?"

"That and . . . well it's a pretty powerful position to be in to refuse to be cooperative in something that means so much to your wife, and, I think, to you too. I wonder if resisting your wife in this is a way of getting back at her."

"For what?"

"What's your theory about that?" I asked him.

"Well . . . it does bother me sometimes, the way she pressures me. It's like she doesn't want me to have a different opinion from hers! Like she makes me wrong for feeling differently . . . especially when she got pregnant before and was so upset because I wasn't as happy as she was about it . . . it wasn't that I didn't want the baby. I just didn't want it as much as she did and she wouldn't let me have that!" he said.

"I know," I said. "And resisting the process of trying to have another baby now is a really effective way of getting back at her and asserting your power. But the only problem is that you have to give up your dreams of having a child too. And that seems like a pretty big sacrifice to me."

"Yeah," he agreed. "But I don't see what I can do about it . . . I've let her have her way on everything else. If I give up on this one I won't have a leg to stand on."

"I know . . . but maybe if you started claiming more power in those other things you wouldn't have to hold on to this one so hard," I suggested.

In our remaining sessions together Carl and I focused on the practical ways in which he could try to begin asserting himself more directly with his wife. At the same time, in couples' therapy he began to speak up about a variety of issues related to their life together—including whether they should move and how much both of them needed to be working if they did move. He and I talked about what it was like for him to begin doing this with his wife and what kinds of fears it brought up for him.

He expressed a great deal of guilt about "doing what his dad could never do," which was to claim his own authority in relation to his wife. He also talked about the sadness he felt about the two babies he had "already lost": one through abortion and the other through miscarriage. And the father who seemed lost to him due to his inaccessibility. It touched a very raw nerve in him to remember how, time and time again, his own father had failed to come to his rescue.

"I remember laying facedown on my bed after being sent to my room for doing something really trivial like talking back to my mother in a snotty tone of voice . . . and I'd be trying really hard to hold back my tears and pounding my fist on the bed over and over again . . . and I'd just be laying there praying for my dad to come home and offer to take me out for a ride . . . anything to get me out of there! A couple of times he did that. Just he and I would go for a long ride until my mom cooled down. We never talked much but I felt real safe there with him. Most of the time he didn't come home until long after I was in bed . . . he just wasn't there

... and that's what I feel like I did to my own baby ...just left him to die."

"In a way that might be true," I said. "By choosing not to be involved in the decision about the abortion, you did kind of opt out ... you refused to accept your parental responsibility towards the child you helped to create, and in a way that is like your dad opting out of his responsibility as a father to protect and defend you. But you don't have to go on choosing not to be a responsible parent."

Accepting responsibility for his part in the pregnancy and its termination allowed Carl to stop unconsciously blaming his ex-girlfriend and his current wife for causing the loss of two of his potential offspring. It also made it possible for him to begin to understand how deeply affected by these two events—the abortion and the miscarriage—he had been.

In our therapy sessions he started wondering about what a child of his might look like "if he ever had one." He also told me that he had started becoming more aware of the presence of babies and young children in the public places he went to. Once he told me about how the sight of a father lifting his young child up over his head, as the child screeched in delight, had "touched something inside him that he had not even been aware was there."

The more he talked about these things, the less vehement he was about standing in the way of trying to conceive another baby. He told me that he did not know why, but he was becoming "less opposed" to having a child. Then one day Carl arrived at my office with a big grin on his face.

"You won't believe this!" he said. "We're finally pregnant!"

"Congratulations!" I said. "I'm delighted for you both. And this time, I see, you're determined not to be left out."

"No way," he said. "She may get sick of me hovering over her, making sure she takes care of herself right. But I'll be there, this time. All the way through. I have to be. For him."

"Him?"

"The baby. Or her, of course," he said. "If it's a girl."

"That's funny," I said. "When you said you had to be there for him I thought you were talking about yourself as a kid, for some reason."

He considered this a moment and replied, "Yeah. For him too."

Men whose partners have had pregnancy losses or abortions often tend to feel left out of the experience, or unentitled to intense feelings about them. There is clearly a sense in which being left out is a physical necessity, since the woman is the one in whose body pregnancies are gestated. And of course there is no inevitable tie between the physical and psychological experiences of pregnancy for men, the way there is for women. But many men are, in fact, becoming closely identified with the pregnancies they help to create and are quite emotionally involved when those pregnancies end prematurely.

Because it is not socially acceptable for men to have intense reactions to these events, however, it is typical for them to dissociate from their feelings about the baby who was lost. They tend to feel it is not their place to grieve deeply for their loss, or even to have their own voice heard in the decision-making process about a particular pregnancy.

This means that men's losses cannot be consciously dealt with but are often "acted out" instead. Carl's disappointment in being left out of the decision with regard to his girlfriend's abortion caused him to withdraw from his wife when she experienced a miscarriage, and to refuse to participate in her continued efforts to have another baby. I have known other men in my practice who have discovered many years after an abortion that they still carry a great deal of grief over this kind of loss. There is simply no place for them to speak about it. Because of this, the particular hopes and dreams the lost baby represented may be more difficult to uncover. But men, like women, need to seek out opportunities to remember, honor and speak about the pregnancy losses and abortions they are party to. And we all need to listen.

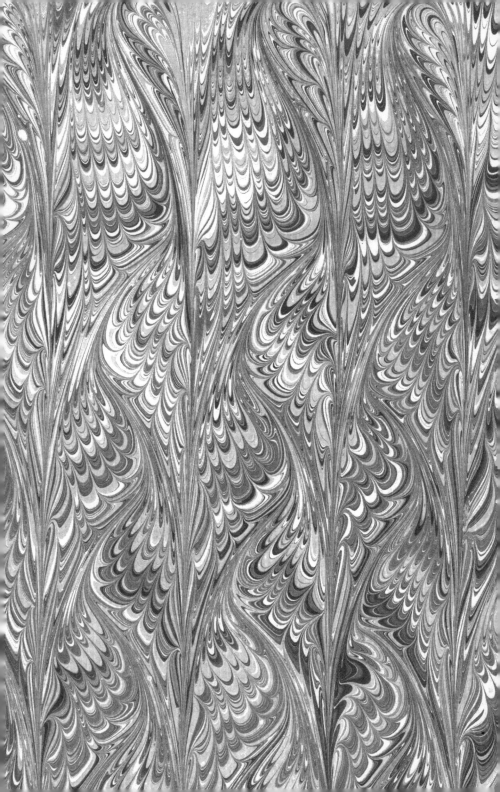

Living with Loss

*I*T WAS *a rainy day and every-one had to cram together in a small meeting room instead of being able to wander freely through the gardens, finding a private corner in which to work. We were all together in that overheated room, so many of us that when my husband and I had arrived there were no seats left and we had to find a place to sit on the floor in the oddly silent room. Having gotten lost on the way to the Zen Center—it was our first visit there—we arrived at the end of the priest's instructions for preparing the tiny red bib we were to place around the neck of the Jizo statue of our choice in the ceremony that would follow.*

All I knew was that this Jizo ceremony was for anyone who had lost a baby through abortion, miscarriage, or death after birth, and that it was intended to honor both those who had died and those who were still living. The flyer had advised us to bring a small piece of red cloth, scissors, a needle and some red thread.

On the stairlike altar which had been set up at the far end of the room there were small statues of bald-headed men in flowing robes, their rounded cheeks and closed eyes reminiscent of sleeping babies.

There were at least a dozen or so of these Jizo statues made of clay and wood and stone, in a variety of shapes and sizes ranging from several inches to nearly a foot in height. There were also other figures: a madonna, a carving that looked like it might be Eskimo art and several others of unidentifiable origin.

We were told that we were each to make a small bib, cape or hat out of the cloth we had brought with us. During the ceremony we would hang our hand-sewn garments around the neck of the Jizo symbol of our choice. Jizo, we were told, is the Buddhist guardian of souls—especially children—in their transit from this world to the next. We could tuck a little note to our lost children inside the pocket of the bib or in the rim of the hat.

I watched as a woman across from us embroidered an intricate design on a tiny red bib she was constructing. The man sitting next to her was carefully winding some thin red cord into tiny tassels. As he finished each one, he carefully handed them to her to sew on the four corners of the bib. I was surprised to see that there were nearly as many men as women here, all silently absorbed in their work.

A young woman in her twenties was sewing a miniature red cape with an older woman who appeared to be her mother. Two women in their thirties huddled closely together, silently consulting on the material they should use for their hat. A hugely pregnant woman was leaning back on her husband's chest as she pulled a long strand of thread through the bib, back and forth, back and forth.

It was odd to be in a room so crowded and yet so quiet. The only sounds were the blowing of noses from the congestion caused by our tears and the soft shuffle of stockinged feet brushing the hardwood floor as one person after another made their way to the altar to make sure their tiny garments fit.

As I watched them, the room began to swim: for a moment, I thought I was going to lose consciousness. But as I drew in a deep breath I realized that I hadn't been breathing: without knowing it, I had been holding my breath. Just as I had held my breath when I was pregnant and knew I was starting to bleed. Holding my *breath, staying very still, trying desperately to hold on.*

Not everyone here had been through exactly what I had been. Some were here because of abortions, some because of miscarriages. Others had experienced stillbirths or the death of their babies shortly after delivery. Our experiences were not identical but they had a common form. And as I looked around I realized that I was probably not the only one feeling light-headed. We had all probably been holding our breath, many of us for a very long time. We were there trying to learn how to let it go.

Jizo is a Japanese Buddhist deity whose special task it is to help protect and care for children. Traditionally, Japanese parents have set up small statues representing their children for Jizo to watch over. More recently, many people have started setting up Jizo statues at their temples, in their homes, and in their communities to represent their miscarried, aborted or stillborn babies. Due to the large increase in the number of abortions in Japan since World War II and the corresponding liberalization of abortion laws,[1] many temples have tried to alleviate the distress of those who have had abortions by providing "mizuko kuyo," the Japanese name for rituals or ceremonies honoring children who die during pregnancy. These Jizo ceremonies have grown enormously in Japan in recent years and have become a major service of the Buddhist temples in Japan.[2] William LaFleur, in his fascinating examination of the function of Jizo ceremonies in Japanese culture, *Liquid Life: Abortion and Buddhism in Japan,* explains:

> *[The] Jizo image can do double service. On the one hand it can represent the soul of the mizuko [the deceased child or fetus] for parents who are doing rites of apology to it. At the same time, the Jizo is also one to whom can be made an appeal or prayer to guide the child or fetus through the realm of departed souls"[3]*

The term "mizuko," applied exclusively to fetuses and children who die early, literally means "children of the waters."[4] In our collective unconscious, water has a deeply resonant meaning: it is from water that life emerges and into water that everything eventually flows. Even our current scientific understanding of the origins of life on earth refers to the "primordial waters" as the environment which nourished the first forms of microscopic life. Water is associated with maternity in general and in particular with the amniotic fluid which provides the warm, fluid environment for the developing fetus. Birth, of course, is the time when the amniotic sack of waters is broken and the baby enters the world.

In the Japanese conception, the "mizuko" is one who "has gone quickly from the warm waters of the womb to another state of liquidity."[5] The life that exists during pregnancy, then, is a "liquid life": a life that is in the process of taking on its own distinctively human form but that could just as easily revert to its former state of pure liquidity. Mizuko, those babies who die during pregnancy or slightly thereafter, are beings who never completely solidify.

This view of life in the womb as something which comes progressively into existence—rather than at a particular moment in time—provides Japanese Buddhists with a different way to answer the question so prominent in Western minds: At what moment does life begin? Part of our dilemma is the contradiction between the idea that abortions performed in early pregnancy have nothing to do with ending a life and the undeniably grief-stricken reactions of many women who have miscarriages at the same gestational age. On the other hand, it seems equally inaccurate and misleading to regard embryonic life as identical to the fully formed life of a newborn, or to try arbitrarily to choose a particular moment in development when human life begins. The idea that life might come progressively into being seems to fit better with the physical fact of the gradual development of life within the womb as well as with the psychological facts of the parents' "psychic" gestation.

The Buddhist view of life in the womb, as described by LaFleur, suggests that a life which ends before birth reverts to a liquid state rather than disappearing entirely, and that it may re-form at some point in the future, possibly even return to its parents and family at a later time. This notion of the possibility of a return—of some sense in which a developing life which never fully came into being may not be lost forever—is enormously comforting to anyone experiencing the torment of the loss of a developing life or trying to reconcile themselves to the need to terminate that life. In this way Japanese Buddhists have found a way to affirm the comforting view that "life might be recalled . . . from the great ocean of being. The cold primeval waters . . . are in fact a warm matrix that is fecund with new life."[6]

There is very little in the way of ritual, tradition, or collective belief in contemporary American culture to help console those who have lost babies during pregnancy or to assist them in the process of coming to terms with their loss. We have no common agreement about the nature of life in the womb and no word for beings who are lost in pregnancy through miscarriage, stillbirth or abortion. This is not surprising, given the deep rift between the two opposing sides in the current debate over abortion. The word "fetus"—which connotes an alien and not necessarily human form of life—tends to be used by the pro-choice movement to refer to all forms of life in the womb, while the right-to-life movement tends to use the word "baby" to refer to even embryonic forms of human life. In contrast, the Japanese term "mizuko," which encompasses all life lost in the womb, acknowledges a connection between fertilized human embryos and full-term babies. It also recognizes the similarities between miscarried and aborted beings, and affirms the idea that losing a pregnancy transcends the particular circumstances of whether or not the loss was chosen. There is no Western equivalent to the Japanese "mizuko kuyo," ceremonies and rituals intended to honor and provide for the well-being of these departed beings, which in many ways provide a deep sense of reassurance to those who have suffered miscarriages, abortions and stillbirths.

There is an implicit belief in our culture that it is not psychologically healthy to dwell on one's sorrows—that what is expected and admirable in people who face setbacks and losses of any kind is to forget about them as quickly as possible and to move on with their lives. To refuse, in essence, to be held back by them. There is a formidable though unconscious fear in our culture that looking back at one's losses, failures or disappointments will condemn one to eternal sorrow—like Orpheus, who lost his one chance to rescue his dead wife from the underworld when he could not help but look back at her.

The idea that there are significant limitations on our ability to control our lives is threatening in a society like ours, which tends to confuse political freedom with psychological freedom. In America, we are free. But the freedom we feel entitled to seems to extend well beyond the Bill of Rights. We believe that we are also free to do, be or feel anything we choose to do, be or feel. It is all just a matter of positive thinking, mind over matter, hard work and determination. Dwelling on the past, we believe, will only slow us down, encumber us, stop us from achieving our goals.

But the fact of the matter is that it does not encumber us to look back on our losses, but actually frees us to move forward in our lives. Of course an endless preoccupation with the sorrows of the past *can* be a way of avoiding the difficulties of the present. But for the most part, our fear of getting stuck if we look back too long is wildly out of proportion to the danger that looking back actually poses. The more pressing danger is in never looking back at all. When we disown important life experiences, we lose a part of ourselves. Facing loss directly allows us to let go of the past and *genuinely* move on, in a way that refusing to look back never does.

Public ceremonies such as funerals and memorial services are ways of assisting people, with the support of their community, to stay conscious of their feelings, no matter how painful. Making grief public and thereby important makes it more bearable. It helps the bereaved to tolerate and accept the reality of loss—a much more difficult task than pretending that the person is only temporarily absent.

Often, people whose loved ones have died cannot fully believe the person is actually dead for quite some time afterward. Sometimes they never do. They refuse to look back when someone close to them dies. They know the person is dead, but on another level, they do not know it at all. A large part of them still believes that if they turn around that person will still be there.

Working through a significant loss involves accepting the reality of the death and making peace with it. It does not mean no longer feeling sad about the death, or never wishing for the person to return or longing for things to be different. It just means no longer protecting oneself from the devastating knowledge of that person's eternal absence.

Memorial services serve the important psychological function of helping mourners to begin to accept the reality of their loss. When a baby dies before birth, such a public ceremony rarely takes place. Although it has become more commonplace in recent years for hospital staff to offer parents the opportunity to view the body of their stillborn babies and to assist them in making arrangements for a formal burial, cremation or memorial service, almost never are accommodations of this kind made for miscarriages, abortions or ectopic pregnancies, and once the procedure is over and the bleeding stops, the incident is thought to be over. In many cases, therefore, the reality of the loss never completely sinks in—there is nothing concrete to point to that has been lost—and little or no consolation or comfort is obtained from others. Rather than being made public and important, the loss can become a private and nameless torment.

It is not possible to have a reproductive crisis which results in a miscarriage, stillbirth or abortion and not have feelings about it that need to be expressed. It is certainly true that the life-altering potential of any particular event varies considerably from person to person, just as the personal significance of any loss varies. An early miscarriage quickly followed by several successful pregnancies may not have the emotional impact of a miscarriage which is followed by years of infertility. But when the social environment is unreceptive to the emotional aftereffects of pregnancy loss, it is much more typical for the feelings, thoughts and reactions to these events to be repressed rather than to be consciously processed, and for the experience itself to become disowned.

Part of the task of the psychotherapist is to provide a container or, in the words of the late British pediatrician and psychoanalyst D. W. Winnicott, "facilitating environment,"[7] in which an awareness and expression of these difficult feelings can take place: a place where the patient can be heard. This requires the therapist to be *willing to listen* to whatever distressing feelings the patient needs to become cognizant of, and to be able to point out the ways in which that awareness is being unconsciously avoided by the patient.

My own experience losing pregnancies certainly helped me learn how to listen better. If I had not struggled to come to terms with my own losses, I am certain I would have dismissed the claim of my patient Rebecca* that her dream about the drowning baby was related to the miscarriage she had several years before. I might well have concluded that her insistence on interpreting the dream in this way was a result of her unconscious desire to avoid becoming aware of how desperate she still felt about her abandonment by her ex-husband. I had learned, after all, from the time I was ten years old standing outside my mother's bathroom door, that one does not speak of miscarriages. And before my own losses taught me differently, I had always assumed that once they were over, *there was nothing more to say* about these unseen losses.

---

* Rebecca's experience is discussed in Chapter Two.

What I discovered when I started really listening to what other people had to say about their own pregnancy losses and abortions was that the most important issue in determining the severity of the impact of any particular loss is not how far along in the pregnancy it occurs (or even whether the loss was chosen or not) but *what kinds of hopes, dreams and fantasies were wrapped around that child.* That is to say, the emotional impact of any particular loss has to do with the quality and degree of attachment to the unborn child: with what the pregnancy unconsciously signifies for the individual person. In some cases, a strong attachment can be formed quite early in the pregnancy or even long before the baby is conceived, while in others the bond may not exist until long after the baby is born. That is why general assumptions about the impact of any particular loss—based on the length of gestation or whether or not the loss was chosen—are likely to be wrong. It is impossible to gauge the depth of the grief by either the size of the coffin or the circumstances of the loss.

I was not certain that Rebecca had been deeply attached to the very early pregnancy she had lost, but my willingness to entertain the possibility that she had been made it possible for us to explore the issue in therapy. When we did so we found that her pregnancy had a great deal of significance for her. The baby held the unconscious promise that she could finally make reparations for her own childhood abandonments by her mother: that she could undo the past in a sense, by providing her child—and vicariously her self—with the kind of security she'd never had. When the baby died and her marriage simultaneously collapsed, Rebecca felt that this promise had been shattered. It left her unable to move forward in her life, unable to risk involvement in another relationship due to a profound fear of another abandonment. Her unconscious "explanation" for the loss of her baby was her own shortcomings.

When Rebecca began to remember and talk about the details of her miscarriage and what it had signified for her, she was finally able to reconcile herself to the loss of an important hope. On the anniversary of her baby's due date Rebecca bought a tiny ring with a small amethyst stone—her baby's birthstone. She also had the baby's name—Melissa—and the date of her miscarriage hand-lettered by a calligrapher so that she could frame it and hang it on her wall at home. Making this nameplate, she told me, was a way of giving her loss more substance. "People who hadn't known about my miscarriage would visit me and see the name and date on the wall and ask me about it," Rebecca told me. "It was much more out in the open that way. I wanted people to know."

Even though the stillbirth of Matthew's* firstborn son was more generally recognized as both significant and real than Rebecca's early loss, Matthew had to struggle just as hard to come to terms with it. The reality of the loss seemed unquestionable: there was a full-term baby delivered, a body he could have chosen to view, and a funeral service which involved the burial of a coffin the size of a shoe box. But it was still extremely difficult for him to make conscious sense of this wholly unexpected and seemingly unnatural event, and for many years it was simply too much to absorb.

After the stillbirth Matthew and his wife hardly spoke about the incident, nor did many of the people around them. In a sense, there was nothing to talk about. No one wanted to bring up the subject for fear of causing them pain, so after a while they did not bring it up and neither did Matthew or his wife, and the silence between them grew. With no safe place to grieve, to let the full impact of his son's death sink in, Matthew repressed the experience and virtually all of the feelings accompanying it.

This way of coping, this turning away from the loss and not looking back, was successful for Matthew in the sense that it protected him from the overwhelming pain of the loss of his firstborn son, but it had its downside too, the worst aspect of which was

---

*Matthew's experience is discussed in Chapter Three.

probably the intense "flashback" experiences he started having ten years later when his daughter was born and the sleepless anxiety he experienced. Matthew had a choice to make then: either he could try to exert even more energy into keeping the experience of his son's death more deeply repressed (and find a way to live with the intense fears about his daughter's well-being), or he could begin to allow himself to remember the experience of his son's death and put his feelings about that trauma into words, thereby both owning and integrating it into his conscious life.

The more difficult course was the latter, but he chose to do so by writing about it in an eloquent article he later published. His daughter's unprompted visit to his son's grave site, her fearless curiosity about her brother, helped to underline the fact that such visits to the past were indeed possible to bear. It was through this internal work that Matthew was able to finally know that he had a son who died, and thus to bring back to life a part of himself.

For Candace,* there was no burial, no funeral service and no sympathy cards after her late-term genetic abortion. And although she went through a painful labor and delivery, she never saw her daughter afterward. The whole experience had a nightmarish quality to it: terrifyingly real but utterly incomprehensible.

Candace was helped tremendously by two things. One was speaking about her own experience with genetic abortion *in the presence of* others who had also had the experience. In this atmosphere of acceptance and compassion, she could begin to reconcile her view of herself as a moral person with the fact of the abortion she had chosen: to find for herself the morality in the decision she had made. She was able to recognize herself in the compassionate and caring people she saw around her, and finally to see herself as being entitled to her grief.

The other thing Candace did, at the suggestion of one of the group members, was to spend several months making a hand-sewn

---

* Candace's experience is discussed in Chapter Four.

doll in honor of her daughter: a rag doll with fine features and an exquisitely detailed smock. She kept the doll on the pillow at the head of her bed and every time she looked at it, she said she felt both "sad and glad." Sad because she would never see her little girl holding that doll. Glad because she had made something so beautiful for her.

In Japan, when parents visit their Jizo statues, they often leave children's toys. These kinds of gestures, like Candace's handmade doll, help would-be parents reconcile their view of themselves as caring people with the harsh reality of having chosen not to bring a developing life into the world. William LaFleur describes the process this way:

> *The terrible fact of abortion makes it all that more important for the parent of the fetus to find concrete evidence that she or he still remains a person who cares and has human feelings.*[8]

We all need recognition by other people of the things that happen to us in our lives, to help us make sense of them and bear them more easily. This is especially true of the traumas, setbacks, illnesses and losses we suffer. By talking about these losses, by hearing the words of others, by seeing our own sorrow reflected in their eyes, we can achieve an important affirmation of our own experience. When other people are reluctant to listen to us, when there are no ceremonies to publicly acknowledge the impact of our experiences, when we do not hear other people talking about similar experiences, we receive the covert message that others *would rather not hear what we have to say*, and this makes it difficult to even identify our reactions to our losses.

A kind of internal censoring process takes place, which alienates us from our own experiences. Arthur Frank, in his autobiographical account of facing first a heart attack and then cancer, describes a similar censoring process that often takes place in response to our culture's discomfort with the psychological trauma of life-threatening illnesses.

> *When I face someone who does not seem willing or able to help me work toward what I might eventually say (about my experience of illness, crisis or loss) I become mute. A person who finds no one willing to take the time and offer the help necessary to bring forth speech will protect himself by saying nothing.* [9]

But when we face great losses, great life-altering events, we need to talk. We need to talk in order to recognize and understand what we are experiencing. We need to talk to come to terms consciously with the traumas of our lives, rather than unconsciously reacting in response to them. We need to talk so that we can learn to live with our inevitable losses and the finite nature of our lives.

We are creatures who inhabit bodies that age, decay and eventually stop working altogether. We fool ourselves by pretending otherwise—by pretending that we can outwit or indefinitely delay death by any number of medical or spiritual techniques. But when our bodies fail us, when they refuse to comply with our wills—when we become ill, for instance, or pregnant when we don't want to be; when we cannot become pregnant when we want to be; or when a baby dies, or is developing abnormally—we are suddenly face-to-face with the immutable fact of our limited control over our bodies and our lives. And no matter how much we may *will* it to be otherwise, all of us, in the end, succumb to the frailties that flesh is heir to.

Just as surely as we have come into existence, we are all passing out of that existence—the process is inevitable and intrinsic to life itself. We have a choice, though, about how to react to this knowledge of our own limitations: we can go on pretending they are not there, or we can try to continue to live with the conscious awareness of those limitations and not be paralyzed by that knowledge. The second choice gives us a deeper appreciation for the fragility of life in general, and it allows us to accompany those we love and care for in the difficult task of facing their own inevitable agonies.

Coming to terms with my own pregnancy losses and the eventual loss of the ability to bear any more children required me to find a way to tolerate living with the heartache rather than endlessly railing in protest against the injustice of my fate. Only when I began to truly accept the reality of these losses, and the lifelong limitations they implied, was I able to genuinely move on in my life and discover the ways in which I was not limited. Also, in learning to tolerate my own distress I became able, as a psychotherapist and as a friend, to accompany others in facing their own despair without needing to run away, or to subtly encourage them to do so.

Part of how I was able to work through my own losses was by remembering the details of every doctor's visit, every trip to the hospital emergency room. I did not want to remember these things. I could not see the point: the memories only brought up sorrow, rage, and a terrible sense of impotence. My impulse was to put it all behind me and never look back. But remembering what happened—by writing about it in detail as it came back to me and by letting myself be aware of the sadness I felt on the anniversaries of my former due dates—made it possible for me to slowly become conscious of all that I had experienced. It was my way of reclaiming, from the deep well of my unconscious, not only my own pregnancy losses but the miscarriages of my mother and my old college friend.

What also helped was attending the Jizo ceremony and several other, more private, ceremonies my husband and I held. The first one we had was on the due date of our first ectopic-pregnancy baby, whom we lost at seven weeks' gestation without ever knowing its gender. We both, I think, imagined it had been a girl—the perfect companion for our then two-year-old son. We invited our parents and a friend and her husband who had recently suffered a miscarriage. We asked everyone to bring something to symbolize the baby who was gone. My mother read a Haiku poem about a little butterfly hunter who had vanished; and my mother-in-law, who could still vividly recall the miscarriage she had before giving birth to her three sons almost forty-eight years before, brought the newborn bracelet my husband wore home from the hospital. My husband and I read letters we had written for the baby we had tried to conceive for several years, telling her how excited we had been to find out about the pregnancy, and how empty our lives felt without her. Then we planted a plum tree with tiny pink blossoms in our front yard.

We held our second ceremony about five years later, only a few months after our final ectopic pregnancy. At that point we had been trying to have another child for almost six years. There were many months of fertility drugs, two surgeries, six in vitro fertilization attempts. Twice, following several positive pregnancy tests, my HCG levels plummeted and I went into shock after a fallopian tube ruptured and began hemorrhaging. In both cases emergency surgery had to be performed to remove the pregnancy and the fallopian tube. After the last surgery we knew that we were not going to have another baby. Although we had seriously considered adoption, we were so emotionally and financially depleted by that time that we were incapable of pursuing that option. But facing the fact that we would not have any more children was one of the most difficult things I would ever have to do, and I did not want it to pass unnoticed. I wanted to mark this time as a turning point in my own life and in our life as a family: to honor our struggles and our losses, to say farewell to the babies we would never have.

And so on the last day of the year, my husband and I found ourselves on a stretch of windy beach at one of the most beautiful spots on the Pacific Coast. I had written another letter; this time it was addressed to all the babies we would never know, telling them how hard we had tried to bring them to life and how sorry we were that we would never know them. I apologized to them for not being able to continue the struggle. My husband talked about the place in his heart that he had prepared that would always be there for them. After I read the letter out loud I folded it into a tiny silver box and he threw the box as far as he could into the rushing surf. As we watched, the waves carried off the box. Then an amazing thing happened: the gentle curve of a huge gray whale rose before us, not a hundred yards from where we stood. When the whale appeared I felt certain our lost children were returning to a place where they belonged, a place where they could be tended to in a way that we no longer found possible. They were returning to the primordial waters. The next day my husband, my son and I spent New Year's Day together, closing the circle of our family.

It has been several years now since we held our private ceremony on that lonely stretch of beach. The sadness hasn't ended, but it has lessened significantly. I have many days when I can see a mother with a new baby and actually pity her for the overwhelming demands of her infant. Often, I can even touch her baby's silky cheek. But it continues to surprise me that the mere sight of a young brother and sister walking home from school together can still bring me to the verge of tears. At some level I am always dimly conscious of the children I wanted who are not here today. But I have learned to be much less afraid of this knowledge, to allow it to come and go as it pleases rather than keeping the door locked tightly against it. I am beginning to regard it as an old friend, a positive sign of the tender affection I held for my dream children rather than a sure sign of my own psychopathology. My longing for more children, for the babies I lost, has not simply gone away. I know now that it never will. What has changed is that I am doing what I never thought possible: little by little, I am learning to live with it. And in doing so I have found a new awareness of the limitations of life, the precariousness of good fortune, and a greater acceptance for what we are given.

Common Experiences Shared by Those Coping with a Reproductive Crisis

Emotional numbing, rage, fearfulness, shame and a continuing sense that one is pregnant are neither abnormal nor uncommon following reproductive crises of all kinds, especially when those losses involve particularly meaningful or precious pregnancies. The degree of trauma following pregnancy loss or abortion varies considerably from case to case, but clearly the loss of a long-wished-for and/or last-chance pregnancy generally involves a great deal more trauma than other pregnancy losses. Difficulty concentrating, thinking clearly, reading, sleeping, relaxing or eating for a period of time immediately following the crisis is neither abnormal nor uncommon, since reproductive crises can be a shock to the system both physically and emotionally.

Emotional numbing and partial memory loss of the events surrounding the crisis seem to be a form of psychological anesthesia which follows traumas of all kinds, and which protects the person from having to cope with the overwhelming nature of the event. Therefore, not feeling anything during and immediately following the event is quite typical. This numbing and/or memory loss can continue for days, weeks or months following the crisis.

Intense rage directed at your partner, doctors, hospital personnel, friends and family or even **at your own body** is a not uncommon reaction to the loss of control over your own destiny that pregnancy loss frequently symbolizes. The potential for rage appears to be greater in cases where the pregnancy was highly valued and its loss was completely beyond the person's control, or was experienced as such. This includes cases of abortion in which the person felt forced into terminating a pregnancy by either other people or life circumstances.

Fearfulness, hopelessness and a sense of vulnerability commonly follow sudden losses of all kinds, and pregnancy losses are no exception. The sudden loss of a precious object—or control over a precious bodily function—may offend your sense of the natural order of things, making the world seem like a foreign place. Feeling weak, unlucky or doomed is also a typical response to sudden loss, as is a sense of forboding or fear of sudden catastrophe. And the more irreplaceable the lost object was, the more shaken you may feel. This fearfulness seems to be more problematic with recurrent losses, or with combined losses such as infertility and pregnancy loss, or IVF failure and pregnancy loss or genetic abortion.

Feelings of remorse, shame and/or the sense of being punished are also normal reactions to a variety of reproductive failures. Self-condemnation for particular personal failings seems to be a way of trying to explain the loss (or the unintended pregnancy) and assign it a clear, hopefully avoidable cause. Unresolved guilt over abortions and pregnancy losses can result in a tendency to behave in a self-destructive manner. Shame is a common accompaniment to many forms of pregnancy loss but can be particularly acute in the case of abortion, and can actually prevent grieving from ever taking place.

It is not uncommon to "feel pregnant" for the duration of an interrupted pregnancy or to temporarily forget that you are no longer pregnant even though you quite consciously know that you are not. This imaginary pregnancy seems to be a form of protective denial which allows the knowledge of the loss to sink in slowly, so that it does not overwhelm the psyche. Dreams about being pregnant and feelings of still being pregnant are often prevalent during this time, especially around the original due date of the lost pregnancy.

Working through the grief caused by significant reproductive crises involves remembering, making your loss real, staying open to your feelings, and finding a place to speak freely.

Remembering involves gradually recalling all the details of what happened before, during and after your crisis. It means not pushing the flashes of memory away when they arise. It means approaching the loss and all the circumstances surrounding it with an accepting, nonjudgmental curiosity which can help you to more consciously come to terms with the loss, and to avoid unconscious guilt and self-punishment. Remembering also includes recalling the particular fantasies you had about the child you lost, the kind of family you would have had, and the kind of parent you imagined yourself to be to that child.

Making your loss real, concrete and tangible can be one of the greatest challenges in coming to terms with it. This seems to be especially true in the case of earlier losses and abortions and in later losses where the baby is not seen. There is something about seeing which makes the loss more tangible and allows grieving to begin. Also, the more unreal the loss seems, the less possible it is to make conscious sense of it and to assimilate the experience as being a part of one's life and identity.

Many people who have lost babies late in pregnancy have reported that seeing, touching and holding their babies is very helpful in this process. Although they may have felt reluctant to do so at first, most are grateful that doctors and nurses gave them the opportunity and, in many cases, encouraged them to see their babies. In cases where this viewing is either impossible or inadvisable (due to the size or condition of the fetus), many have found it helpful to construct something tangible which can come to represent your lost baby in your mind's eye. Some people have made hand-sewn dolls or clay figures or wooden statues. Others have saved photographs of their babies, or ultrasound negatives. Such mementos are a way of both remembering and expressing your caring for your lost child.

Funerals, memorial services and personal rituals or ceremonies—especially when held on important dates such as the baby's due date or an anniversary—can also be helpful in making the loss tangible and significant. When friends, family and/or members of your community are included in these ceremonies they not only can provide you with sorely needed emotional support, but in their acknowledgment of your loss can help to remind you that the loss was a real and grievable event.

Some religious groups have ways of acknowledging and memorializing pregnancy losses, especially stillbirths, but few have ways of acknowledging earlier losses and abortions. Certainly, if you are affiliated with a particular religion it is advisable to inquire about the availability of these special services. But even if none are available, it is entirely possible to design and hold a ceremony of your own which can significantly assist you in the process of working through your loss.

Different kinds of rituals and ceremonies have worked for different people, but there seem to be three basic elements which tend to meet certain universal needs. These elements are **expressing the hopes and dreams held for the baby who was lost, making an offering of some kind in honor of the lost being, and doing something which signifies one's readiness to let go of him or her.**

Expressing the hopes and dreams for the lost baby can be accomplished in the form of a letter written to him or her recalling the wishes you had for that particular child. Calling your child by name, even if you had not settled on a name at the time of the loss or did not know the baby's gender, can also be helpful in this process. You may wish to read your letter out loud to the others at your ceremony and then find a way to symbolically "send it" to your lost child or save it for yourself to refer back to.

Making an offering of some kind in honor of the lost baby can take many different forms. You might want to plant a tree or a bush in their honor, you might want to make a toy or buy a birthstone in honor of the baby's birthdate. Planting a living thing is often felt to be a satisfying substitute for the life that was ended, and when it is planted on the due date it can be a way of marking the end of one life with the beginning of another, and of tracking the passage of time after the loss.

Doing something to signify one's readiness to let go can also take a variety of forms. Releasing balloons, burying mementos, dropping a note in the water, burning medical records related to the loss: all can serve as ways of both caring for and releasing the being who is gone.

Another important part of learning to live with your loss is **staying open to your feelings.** It is better to give yourself the freedom to experience the full range of your emotional response to the loss than to try to block them. Grief comes in waves rather than discreet stages: at first the waves are large ones and you might feel afraid that they will drown you, but they won't. Eventually, they get smaller and more manageable, though they never go away completely. You need to learn how to tolerate the feelings without being knocked over by them. Ironically, the more you are able to consciously process your grief, the less problematic it will become in the future.

Don't be surprised if you get hit with stronger waves of grief around the baby's due date or on anniversaries of either the due date or the date of the loss. It is not uncommon to feel either lethargic or anxious, or to have difficulty concentrating or sleeping. It is also not unusual to feel more compulsive than usual, to have a stronger desire to numb your feelings. In the long run it is better not to resist your sadness or try to hide it from yourself and others. It is quite understandable that you feel grief-stricken; you have experienced a real loss. That intense ache won't last forever, especially if you let yourself remain receptive to whatever emotions arise.

Finding a place where you can speak freely about your loss, where you will be heard and understood, is critical. This place might be in a support group, among sympathetic friends or family members, or in the presence of a psychotherapist, doctor or spiritual leader. But it is important to keep in mind that not everyone will be able to listen. Some may be so uncomfortable with loss in general—or with your particular kind of loss—that they may unwittingly try to silence you by telling you, in so many words, to look on the bright side before you have even been able to talk about the dark side. Don't let this kind of response convince you that you are crazy to be so upset. Just keep looking for the people who can accompany you in this difficult journey. Anyone who has been able to consciously tolerate the pain of any kind of loss can be there for you.

For Family and Friends Whose Loved Ones Are Dealing with a Reproductive Crisis

GRIEVING TAKES TIME

Those who care about someone in a reproductive crisis face two main difficulties. The first is witnessing their loved one's distress and feeling helpless to provide any significant assistance. There is an impulse to try to gloss over the severity of the event, to provide immediate reassurance, in an attempt to cheer the person up. Remarks like "You can always have another one" or "Be thankful for the child (or the marriage or the family or the life) you *do* have" are often intended to console grieving parents, but often what they imply is that they should not be as upset as they are. For this reason, initial remarks of this kind tend to silence those in distress, rather than to assist them in coming to terms with their losses.

Having or adopting other children, finding other outlets for one's procreative impulses (such as tending a garden or raising animals, doing artwork or starting a new business), can ultimately be very healing. The grieving person will, if allowed to fully process the loss, eventually be able to appreciate the riches of his or her life once again. But none of these things is a *solution* for the grief of losing this particular pregnancy. Each loss needs to be mourned in its own way and time in order for true healing to begin.

Grief tends to ebb and flow like the tide. Don't be surprised if the person you care for seems fine one day and devastated the next. Due dates and anniversaries of due dates and losses are times that are likely to be especially difficult for would-be parents. Try not to expect too much from mourners, especially in the weeks immediately following the crisis and around those important times. Also try not to look to them for emotional support at these sensitive times.

It is also important not to expect or demand that the grieving persons recover from their loss as quickly as possible and not to imply that they are abnormal if they suffer more intensely than you think they ought to. Give them time and plenty of space—they've suffered an injury from which they need time to heal.

By the same token, don't worry if they don't seem to be "in touch with their feelings" and are not expressing enough sadness. Everyone processes their grief in their own way and their own time. All you can do is offer, over and over again, to be there when they want you to be.

Don't Withdraw

The other difficulty that often leads to counterproductive behavior is that the people around those in crisis may be so grief-stricken or overwhelmed by the enormity of the event themselves that they cannot provide emotional support for their loved ones or cannot even bear to speak of the event or hear anything about it. Stillbirths or the loss of extremely "precious" pregnancies (long awaited or last-chance or both) may be so horrifying to friends and extended family members that they have difficulty being emotionally present for the bereaved parents. You need to appreciate how deeply affected you have been and seek out help from other sources so that you can continue to be available to your loved ones. If emotional retreat is unavoidable on your part, it is far better to openly acknowledge your difficulty in coping with the loss than to silently withdraw from the person with the rationalization that you don't want to 'intrude on" them by calling them up, initiating contact with them or asking how they are holding up emotionally.

DON'T PERPETUATE THE SILENCE

Avoiding the subject of the loss does not alleviate the suffering. In fact, the reverse is often true: silence is akin to abandonment and it makes the mourner feel isolated and alone. Saying "the wrong thing" is better than saying nothing at all.

Don't take the mourners' hostility too personally. Make allowances for the emotionally raw state they may be in and don't expect them to "be themselves." Grief encompasses rage and outrage, and in most cases that rage has no appropriate target. It may be directed at doctors, nurses, hospital, life in general, or at you.

LISTEN

If you don't have any idea what the person is going through, or what it might be like to experience what they are experiencing, ask them, gently, to tell you about it. Let them know you are available to listen whenever they want to talk. Although this is a great deal easier said than done—it's painful to see them in pain—simply sitting quietly while the person talks or cries, letting them know you are there and you care (and continuing to actively remind the person of your availability to **be with them**) is absolutely the most important way you can help. **So far as you are able, remain present and emotionally available, and be willing to listen.**

Special Notes for Mental Health and Medical Professionals

Don't inadvertently minimize the emotional impact of early losses and abortions. In our culture, these kinds of pregnancy losses are often assumed to carry little emotional weight, and for that reason it can be easy to unintentionally minimize their significance for a particular patient and her partner. Because those in reproductive crises are often overwhelmed by their feelings and look to professionals to verify their shaken view of reality, adopting an attitude which minimizes the event can hinder their efforts to grapple with the full range of emotions the loss may inspire.

Offering and encouraging patients the opportunity to view, touch, hold and/or photograph the fetus whenever feasible is often quite helpful in allowing the grieving process to begin. Few people seem to regret having seen their babies, but many regret not having done so, or not having had the opportunity to do so. Among those I have spoken with, even people who were reluctant to see their babies immediately following the loss, later expressed a great deal of gratitude toward hospital personnel for making this viewing possible and for encouraging them to take advantage of it. This viewing not only tends to make the loss more concrete—and thus initiates conscious grieving—but also gives parents a comforting sense of ongoing connection with their baby, which they seem to treasure as time goes by.

Offering supportive resources—books, Internet Web sites, support groups, referrals to psychotherapists specializing in pregnancy loss, and resources for help in designing ceremonies and memorials—**even to patients who have experienced very early losses, abortions, or "replaceable" losses—can be very helpful.** The cultural silence surrounding these losses may make patients more reluctant to reveal the depth of their reactions to them. The gesture of offering resources gives patients and their partners permission to take their feelings seriously.

Preparing yourself for the fact that misdirected rage may spill over in your direction may make it easier to cope with. Attempting to stay emotionally available for your patients, being **willing to listen** to what they have to say, empathizing with the injustice of their plight and with the difficulty of finding an appropriate target for their anger, are all more helpful to patients and their partners than withdrawing from them.

Encouraging patients to give themselves plenty of time to recover both physically and emotionally before making a decision about a future pregnancy, and **resisting the impulse** to try to "fix" their emotional distress by offering immediate medical solutions or advising them to focus only on a future pregnancy, can help prevent the delay or indefinite postponement of the grieving process. Giving in to patients' pressures to move forward quickly encourages them to avoid their reactions to their current loss, which can negatively affect their relationship with future children.

Assuming that a reproductive crisis was emotionally insignificant just because the patient appears to be taking it in stride can be risky. Some people do seem to be genuinely able to "process" the impact of such events rapidly and effortlessly. However, given the enormous social pressures on patients to minimize the impact of these events, and the further fact that emotional numbing is a common initial reaction to these crises, it is important to remain alert to the possibility that the patient's emotions surrounding the event may have been repressed, dissociated or expressed somatically, and that the grieving process has been stalled.

By the same token, don't assume that all pregnancy losses and abortions cause a significant degree of distress for everyone. The loss of highly prized pregnancies such as those which are long awaited, or those which are likely to be the woman's last chance to have a child, are obviously likely to be much harder to recover from than the chosen loss, say, of a young woman who finds herself accidentally pregnant and can look forward to many more opportunities for bearing a child. The only way to gauge the significance of a particular loss is to take the time to ask about all the relevant circumstances surrounding it.

Guilt and shame may play a large role in preventing patients from working through their grief. This seems to be especially true in the case of pregnancy losses and abortions which took place a long time ago, and also in the cases of very early pregnancy loss and abortions. Creating an atmosphere of unconditional acceptance and compassion is a key factor in assisting these patients.

The overall goal of psychotherapeutic work with patients who have experienced reproductive crises and are struggling to come to terms with them is to help them make conscious sense of their experiences (through remembering in great detail exactly what happened—either in written or spoken words) in order to prevent unconscious dissociation of the experience and lingering, unresolved, shadow grief. In cases where a particularly precious pregnancy has been lost, it is often important to uncover the *unconscious significance* of the event. In cases where, for whatever reason, the loss was never consciously dealt with for many years, it is more likely that a fixed, though unconscious, meaning has been assigned to the loss. Interpretive dream work and free association in psychotherapy are often helpful in uncovering and dispelling these destructive interpretations.

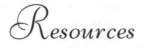

Resources

PREGNANCY LOSS

Organizations

The following organizations provide information and services related to pregnancy loss.

AMEND (Aiding a Mother Experiencing Neonatal Death)
National Headquarters
4324 Berrywick Terrace
St. Louis, MO 63128
(314) 487-7582

There are many chapters of AMEND nationwide.

Association for Recognition of Life of Stillbirths
11128 West Front Ave.
Littleton, CO 80127
(303) 978-9517

Center for Loss in Multiple Births
P.O. Box 1064
Palmer, AK 99645

The Compassionate Friends, Inc.
National Headquarters
P.O. Box 3696
Oak Brook, IL 60522-3696

Compassionate Friends has many chapters
throughout the country.

HAND (Help after Neonatal Death)
P.O. Box 62
San Anselmo, CA 94960
(415) 492-0720

MIDS Inc. (Miscarriage, Infant Death, Stillbirth)
c/o Janet Tischler
16 Crescent Drive
Parsippany, NJ 07054
(201) 966-6437

National Sudden Infant Death Syndrome Foundation
P.O. Box 3044
Oakton, VA 22124-3044
(703) 435-7130

Perinatal Loss Project
2116 N.E. 18th Ave.
Portland, OR 97212-2621
(503) 284-7426

Pregnancy Loss Support Program
National Council of Jewish Women, NY Section
9 East 69th St.
New York, NY 10021

SANDS
(Stillbirth and Neonatal Death Society)
28 Portland Place
London, England W1N 4 DE
(Helpline: 0171 436 5881)

SHARE
(A Source of Help in Airing and Resolving Experiences)
National Headquarters
St. John's Hospital
800 East Carpenter St.
Springfield, IL 62702
(217) 544-6464

SHARE has a nationwide list of support groups and many chapters nationwide. Manuals on starting your own group are also available.

SIDS Alliance (Sudden Infant Death Syndrome)
10500 Little Patuxent Parkway, Suite 420
Columbia, MD 21044
(800) 221-SIDS

Recommended Reading

Friedman, Rochelle, and Bonnie Gradstein. *Surviving Pregnancy Loss: A Complete Sourcebook for Women and Their Families.* Boston: Little, Brown, 1982. rev. ed.

Kohn, Ingrid, and Perry Lynne Moffitt. *A Silent Sorrow: Pregnancy Loss, Guidance and Support for You and Your Family.* New York: Dell Publishing, 1992.

Kohner, Nancy, and Alix Henley. *When A Baby Dies: The Experience of Late Miscarriage, Stillbirth and Neonatal Death.* London and San Francisco: HarperCollins, 1991.

Panuthos, Claudia, and Catherine Romeo. *Ended Beginnings: Healing Childbearing Losses.* New York: Warner Books, 1984.

Peppers, Larry, and Ronald Knapp. *How to Go on Living after the Death of a Baby.* Atlanta: Peachtree Publishers, 1993.

ABORTION AND GENETICS

Organizations

Alliance of Genetic Support Groups
1001 22nd. St. NW., Suite 800
Washington, DC 20037
(800) 336-GENE

National Abortion Federation
1436 U St. NW, Suite 103
Washington, DC 20009
(202) 667-5881

Consumer Hotline: (800) 772-9100

National Abortion Rights Action League
1101 14th St. NW, Suite 500
Washington, DC 20005
(202) 408-4600

March of Dimes Birth Defects Foundations
1275 Mamaroneck Ave.
White Plains, NY 10605
(914) 428-7100

National Down Syndrome Congress
1800 Dempster
Park Ridge, IL 60068-1146
(800) 232-6372

Planned Parenthood Federation of America
810 Seventh Ave.
New York, NY 10019
(212) 541-7800

Project Rachel
National Office of Post-Abortion Reconciliation and Healing
Support
3501 South Lake Drive
P.O. Box 07477
Milwaukee, WI 5307-0477
(414) 483-4141

National Society of Genetics Counselors
233 Canterbury Drive
Wallingford, PA 19086
(215) 872-7608

Recommended Reading

Bonavoglia, Angela, ed. *The Choices We Made: 25 Women Speak Out about Abortion.* New York: Random House, 1991.

Carey, Peter. "A Small Memorial," *The New Yorker,* Sept. 25, 1995, pp. 54–63.

DePuy, Candace, and Dana Dovitch. *The Healing Choice: Your Guide to Emotional Recovery after an Abortion.* New York: Simon and Schuster, 1996.

Kushner, Eve. *Experiencing Abortion: A Weaving of Women's Words.* Binghamton, New York: Haworth Press, 1997.

Nathanson, Sue. *Soul Crisis: One Woman's Journey through Abortion to Renewal.* New York: Signet, 1990.

Publications on abortion and Catholicism are also available through Catholics for a Free Choice (202) 986-6093 and The Hope Clinic for Women (800) 844-3130.

INFERTILITY

Organizations

RESOLVE, INC.
National Headquarters
1310 Broadway
Somerville, MA 02144
(617) 623-0744

RESOLVE is a nonprofit organization which assists people struggling with infertility by providing information, referrals and support groups. There are hundreds of chapters across the United States. Call the national headquarters to obtain assistance in locating the one nearest you.

American Fertility Society
2140 11th Ave. South, Suite 200
Birmingham, AL 35205
(205) 933-8494

Recommended Reading

Harkness, Carla. *The Infertility Book: A Comprehensive Medical and Emotional Guide.* Berkeley, California: Celestial Arts, 1992.

Fleming, Anne Taylor. *Motherhood Deferred: A Woman's Journey.* New York: G. P. Putnam's Sons, 1994.

Salzer, Linda P. *Surviving Infertility: A Compassionate Guide through the Emotional Crisis of Infertility.* New York: HarperPerennial, 1991.

INTERNET

GriefNet:
Discussion and support groups for all forms of bereavement including pregnancy loss.

http://rivendell.org:80/

Hygeia: An Online Journal for Pregnancy and Neonatal Loss

http://www.connix.com/hygeia

Miscarriage Support and Information Resources:
Includes newsgroups for support on pregnancy loss and both primary and secondary infertility; mailing lists; websites; and books.

http://www.pinelandpress.com/support/miscarriage

H.A.N.D. (Houston's Aid in Neonatal Death):
Support for parents who have lost babies from conception to late infancy.

http://www.hem.org/hand

Hannah's Prayer:
Christian infertility and pregnancy loss group

http://www.hannah.org/loss.htm

National SHARE Office:
Pregnancy and infant loss support.

http://www.NationalSHAREOffice.com

Pen Parents Inc.:
International nonprofit support network for bereaved parents. Includes losses from miscarriage to the death of adult children.

http://www.angelfire.com/nv/penparents

Personal Stories of Loss:
A collection of stories of all types of losses contributed by readers.

   http://wdg.mc.duke.edu/brook006/stories.html

RESOLVE:
A national nonprofit organization which assists people in resolving their infertility through information, support and advocacy.

   http://www.resolve.org

SANDS:
Support for those who have experienced pregnancy losses, miscarriages, stillbirths or neonatal deaths.

   http://members.aol.com/babyloss/sands.html

Women in Transition:
A post-abortion support group, nonprofit and nondenominational.

   http://www.wits.org

Notes

Preface

[1] From "Three Women: A Poem for Three Voices" in *The Collected Poems of Sylvia Plath*, edited by Ted Hughes (New York: Harper & Row, 1981), p. 187.

Chapter One

[1] *Statistical Abstract of the United States: 1996* (116th ed.), no. 109, *Pregnancies, Number and Outcome: 1976-92* (Washington, D.C.: U.S. Bureau of the Census, 1996), p. 83.

[2] John Bowlby, *Attachment and Loss*, vol. 3: *Loss* (New York: Basic Books, 1980), p. 234.

[3] Ibid., p. 236.

Chapter Two

[1] M. Esther Harding, *The Way of All Women: A Psychological Interpretation* (New York: Harper & Row, 1970), p.160.

[2] Quoted by Laura Chester, ed., in *Cradle and All: Women Writers on Pregnancy and Birth* (New York: Faber & Faber, 1989), p. 2.

[3] Jeanne Menary, "The Amniocentesis-Abortion Experience: A Study of the Psychological Effects and Healing Process" (Ph.D. diss., Harvard University, 1987), p. 87.

[4] Excerpted from an interview conducted by Dr. Jeanne Menary. Ibid., p. 95.

[5] Ingrid Kohn and Perry-Lynn Moffitt, *A Silent Sorrow: Pregnancy Loss, Guidance and Support for You and Your Family* (New York: Dell, 1992), p. 69.

6 Ibid.

7 Ibid., *A Silent Sorrow,* p. 84.

8 Sharon Begley, "The Baby Myth," *Newsweek,* September 4, 1995, p. 40. Source: Panak.

9 Kohn and Moffitt, *A Silent Sorrow,* p. 334.

10 Bowlby, *Attachment and Loss,* vol. 3: *Loss,* pp. 41–43.

11 Control mastery theory, originated by Drs. Harold Sampson and Daniel Weiss for the San Francisco Psychoanalytic Research Group, is very instructive on this point. For more information, see Lewis Engel and Tom Ferguson, *Imaginary Crimes: Why We Punish Ourselves and How to Stop* (Boston: Houghton Mifflin, 1990).

Chapter Three

1 From "Three Women: A Poem for Three Voices," in *The Collected Poems of Sylvia Plath,* edited by Ted Hughes (New York: Harper & Row, 1981), p. 176.

2 Patrick Henry, "Terrorism," *North West Magazine, The Oregonian,* August 25, 1985, p. 21.

3 Source: *Statistical Abstract of the United States, 1995* (Washington, D.C.: U.S. Department of Commerce and Bureau of the Census).

4 *Statistical Abstract of the United States, 1995.*

5 Anaïs Nin, in "Birth," from *Under a Glass Bell* (London: Peter Owen Ltd., 1948).

6 Sylvia Vegetti Finzi, *Mothering: Toward a New Psychoanalytic Construction* (New York: Guilford Press, 1996).

7 Henry, "Terrorism."

8 S. Bourne, "The Psychological Effects of Stillbirth on Women and Their Doctors," *Journal of Research Collections for General Practitioners* 16: 103–12.

9 E. Lewis, "Management of a Stillbirth: Coping with an Unreality,"

The Lancet, September 18, 1976, pp. 619–20.

[10] American Psychological Association, *Diagnostic and Statistical Manual of Psychiatric Disorders,* 4th ed. (Washington, D.C., 1994), pp. 424–29.

[11] Henry, "Terrorism."

Chapter Four

[1] From "The Road Not Taken," in *The Poetry of Robert Frost,* edited by Edward Connery Lathem, (New York: Henry Holt, 1969).

[2] *Statistical Abstract of the United States: 1996* (116th ed.), no. 109, *Pregnancies Number and Outcome: 1976–92* (Washington, D.C.: U.S. Bureau of the Census, 1996), p. 83.

[3] For more information on this topic, see Sigmund Freud's "Beyond the Pleasure Principle" in *The Freud Reader,* ed. Peter Gay (New York: W. W. Norton, 1989), pp. 594–625. The essay was originally published in 1920.

[4] Source: Rachel Benson Gold, *Abortion and Women's Health: A Turning Point for America?* (New York and Washington, D.C.: The Alan Guttmacher Institute, 1990), p. 13.

[5] From Anne Sexton, *Anne Sexton: The Complete Poems* (Boston: Houghton Mifflin, 1981), p. 61–62.

[6] Source: California Department of Health Services, "Risk Table for Chromosomal Abnormalities by Maternal Age at Term" (Berkeley, California: 1995).

[7] ACOG Patient Education, "Maternal Serum Screening for Birth Defects" (Washington, D.C.: American College of Obstetrics and Gynecologists, 1994).

[8] The controversial "partial birth abortion" which Congress passed a bill prohibiting in 1996—subsequently vetoed by President Clinton—actually refers to what is known in the medical community as "intact D&C" and was developed in the 1980s by Dr. James T. McMahon, who was concerned that D&E's per-

formed in the later phases of pregnancy sometimes tore the uterus, causing substantial blood loss, and also involved dismembering the fetus in utero. McMahon's method, which is intended to be used only in cases where the baby's abnormalities are "incompatible with life," involves inserting a needle into the baby's skull and withdrawing fluid so that the baby's head can safely pass through the mother's cervix. Fewer than five hundred such procedures are performed annually in the United States. (Source: Patrice Apodaca, "The Politics of Heartbreak," *Los Angeles Times,* May 7, 1996, Section E, pp. 1 and 6).

9 Patient's Fact Sheet: "Multiple Gestation and Multifetal Pregnancy Reduction" (Montgomery, Alabama: American Society for Reproductive Medicine, 1996).

Chapter Five

1 From "Home Burial," in *The Poetry of Robert Frost,* edited by Edward Connery Lathem (New York: Henry Holt, 1969).

2 One notable exception is a book written by Arthur B. Shostak and Gary McLouth with Lynn Seng, *Men and Abortion: Lessons, Losses and Love* (New York: Praeger Publishers, 1984).

3 See Edith Jacobson, M.D., "Development of the Wish for a Child in Boys," *Psychoanalytic Study of the Child* 5: 139–52.

4 John Wapner, "The Attitudes, Feelings and Behaviors of Expectant Fathers Attending Lamaze Classes," *Birth and Family Journal* 3 (1976): 5–13.

5 Libby and Arthur Coleman, *The Father* (Wilmette, Illinois: Chiron Publications, 1988), p. 129.

6 Excerpted from "Home Burial," *The Poetry of Robert Frost.*

7 Libby Coleman and Arthur Coleman, *Pregnancy: The Psychological Experience* (New York: Seabury Press, 1971), p. 96.

8 Ibid, p. 96.

9 For example, Bob Shacochis, "Missing Children: One Couple's Anguished Attempt to Conceive," *Harper's* (October 1996): 55–63;

Keven Canty, "Death before Life," *Vogue* (May 1995): 93–96; Hillel S. Bromberg, "Lost Fathers: Men and Miscarriage," *Utne Reader* (November/December 1993): 96–97.

ChapterSix

[1] Paul Sachdev, "Abortion Trends: An International Review," *International Handbook on Abortion* (New York: Greenwood Press 1988), p. 8.

[2] William LaFleur, *Liquid Life: Abortion and Buddhism in Japan* (Princeton, N.J.: Princeton University Press, 1992), p. 4.

[3] LaFleur, *Liquid Life,* p. 8

[4] Ibid., p. 16

[5] Ibid.

[6] Ibid., p. 29.

[7] D. W. Winnicott, *Playing and Reality* (London and New York: Routledge, 1986), p. 141. Originally published by Tavistock Publications Ltd. in 1971.

[8] LaFleur, *Liquid Life,* p. 155.

[9] Arthur W. Frank, *At the Will of the Body* (Boston: Houghton Mifflin, 1991), p. 140.

Bibliography

Pregnancy Loss

Borg, Susan, and Judith Lasker. *When Pregnancy Fails: Families Coping with Miscarriage, Stillbirth and Infant Loss.* Rev. ed. Boston: Beacon Press, 1990.

Bromberg, Hillel S. "Lost Fathers: Men and Miscarrage." *Utne Reader* (November/December 1993): 96–97.

Cain, A. C. "On Replacing a Child." *Journal of American Academy of Child Psychiatry* 3 (1964): 443–56.

Canty, Kevin. "Death before Life." *Vogue* (May 1995): 93–96.

Chira, Susan. "Hers: When Hope Died." *New York Times Magazine,* Sunday, June 26, 1994, p. 20.

Costello, Audry, Sandra L. Gardner, and Gerald Merenstein. "Perinatal Grief and Loss." *Journal of Perinatology* 8 (1990): 361–70.

DeFrain, John. *Stillborn: The Invisible Death.* Lexington, Mass.: Lexington Books, 1986.

Ewy, Donna, and Roger Ewy. *Death of a Dream.* New York: E. P. Dutton, 1984.

Faldet, Rachel, and Karen Fitton, eds. *Our Stories of Miscarriage: Healing with Words.* Minneapolis: Fairview Press, 1997.

Fitsch, Julie, with Ilse Sherokee. *The Anguish of Loss: For the Love of Justin.* Long Lake, Minn.: Wintergreen Press, 1988.

Floyd, Cathy Cornwell. "Pregnancy after Reproductive Failure." *The American Journal of Nursing* 81, no. 11 (November 1981): 2050–53.

Friedman, Rochelle, and Bonnie Gradstein. *Surviving Pregnancy Loss: A Complete Sourcebook for Women and Their Families.* Boston: Little, Brown, 1982.

Furlong, Regina M., and John Hobbins. "Grief in the Perinatal Period." *Obstetrics and Gynecology* 81: 1 (1983): 497–500.

Henry, Patrick. "Terrorism." *Oregonian News* (Northwest Magazine), August 25, 1985, p. 21.

Kirksey, Janet, R.N. "Impact of Pregnancy Loss on Subsequent Pregnancy." *Pregnancy Loss: Medical Therapeutics and Practical Considerations.* Baltimore: Williams & Wilkens, 1987.

Knapp, R., and L. Peppers, "Doctor-Patient Relationships in Fetal-Infant Death Encounters." *Journal of Medical Education* 54 (1979): 775–80.

Kohn, Ingrid, and Perry Lynn Moffitt. *A Silent Sorrow: Pregnancy Loss, Guidance and Support for You and Your Family.* New York: Dell Publishing, 1992.

Kohner, Nancy, and Alix Henley. *When a Baby Dies: The Experience of Late Miscarriage, Stillbirth and Neonatal Death.* London and San Francisco: HarperCollins, 1991.

Lewis, Emanuel, M.D. "Inhibition of Mourning by Pregnancy:

Psychopathology and Management" *British Medical Journal* 2 (July 7, 1979): 27–28.

―――. "Mourning by the Family after a Stillbirth or Neonatal Death." *Archives of Diseases in Childhood* 54 (1979): 303–6.

―――. "The Management of Stillbirth: Coping with an Unreality." *The Lancet,* September 18, 1976, pp. 619–20.

Lewis, Emanuel, and Anne Page. "Failure to Mourn a Stillbirth: An Overlooked Catastrophe." *British Journal of Medical Psychology* 51 (1978): 237–41.

Limbo, Rana K., and Sara Rich Wheeler. *When a Baby Dies: A Handbook for Healing and Helping.* La Crosse, Wis.: Resolve Through Sharing, 1986.

Nin, Anaïs. *Under a Glass Bell.* London: Peter Owen Ltd., 1948.

Panuthos, Claudia, and Catherine Romeo. *Ended Beginnings: Healing Childbearing Losses.* New York: Warner Books, 1984.

Peppers, Larry G., Ph.D., and Ronald J. Knapp, Ph.D. *How to Go on Living after the Death of a Baby.* Atlanta: Peachtree Publishers, 1993.

―――. "Maternal Reactions to Involuntary Fetal/Infant Death." *Psychiatry* 43 (1980): 155–59.

Poznanski, Elva O. "The Replacement Child: A Saga of Unresolved Parental Grief." *Journal of Pediatrics* 81 (1972): 1190–93.

Rando, Therese, ed. *Parental Loss of a Child.* Champagne, Ill: Research Press Co., 1986.

Savage, Judith A. *Mourning Unlived Lives: A Psychological Study of Childbearing Loss.* Wilmette, Ill.: Chiron Publications, 1989.

Siebel, M., and W. Graves. "The Psychological Implications of Spontaneous Abortions." *Reproductive Medicine* 24 (1980): 161–65.

Shaw, C. T. "Grief over Fetal Loss." *Family Practice Recertification* 5 (1980): 161–65.

Sherokee, Ilse. *Empty Arms: A Guide to Help Parents and Loved Ones Cope with Miscarriage, Stillbirth and Neonatal Death.* Long Lake, Minn.: 1982.

Sherokee, Ilse, and Linda Hammer Burns. *Miscarriage: A Shattered Dream.* Longlake, Minn.: Wintergreen Press, 1985.

Stack, J. "Spontaneous Abortion and Grieving." *American Family Physician* 21 (1980): 99–102.

Stringham, Jean, Judith Riley, and Ann Ross. "Silent Birth: Mourning a Stillborn Baby." *Social Work* 202, no. 17 (1982): 322–27.

Wolff, John R., M.D., Paul Nielson, M.D., and Patricia Schiller, B.A. "The Emotional Reaction to a Stillbirth." *American Journal of Obstetrics and Gynecology* 108, no. 1 (Sept. 1, 1970): 73–77.

GRIEF

Bowlby, John. *Attachment and Loss,* vol. 3: *Loss (Sadness and Depression).* New York: Basic Books (Division of HarperCollins), 1980.

———. "Processes of Mourning." *International Journal of Psychoanalysis* 42 (1961): 317–40.

Kubler-Ross, Elisabeth, M.D. *On Death and Dying.* New York: Macmillan Publishing Co., 1969.

Lindemann, E. "Symptomatology and Management of Acute Grief." *American Journal of Psychiatry* 101 (1944): 141–48.

Parkes, C. M. "Effects of Bereavement on Physical and Mental Health: A Study of Widows." *British Medical Journal* 2 (1964): 274–79.

Raphael, B. *The Anatomy of Bereavement.* New York: Basic Books, 1983.

Sanders, C. M. "A Comparison of Adult Bereavement in the Death of a Child, Spouse and Parent. *Omega* 10, no. 4 (1979–80): 303–22.

ABORTION

Bonavoglia, Angela, ed. *The Choices We Made: 25 Women Speak Out about Abortion.* New York: Random House, 1991.

Buckels, N. B. "Abortion: A Technique for Working Through Grief." *Journal of American College Health Association* 30 (1982): 181 82.

Carey, Peter. "A Small Memorial." *The New Yorker,* September 25, 1995, pp. 54–63.

Cavanar, J., A. Maltbie, and J. L. Sullivan. "Aftermath of Abortion: Anniversary Reaction and Abdominal Pain." *Bulletin of the Menninger Clinic* 42 (1978): 433–44.

David, H. P. "Psychosocial Studies of Abortion in the U.S."

Abortion in Psychosocial Perspective: Trends in Transnational Research. New York: Springer Publishing (1978): 77–115.

————. "Abortion in Psychological Perspective." *American Journal of Orthopsychiatry* 42, no.1 (January 1972):61–67.

Franckle, L. B. *The Ambivalence of Abortion.* New York: Random House, 1978.

Freeman, Ellen W. "Abortion: Subjective Attitudes and Feelings." *Family Planning Perspectives* 10 (May/June 1978): 150–55.

Gilligan, Carol. *In A Different Voice: Psychological Theory and Women's Development.* Cambridge, Mass., and London: Harvard University Press, 1982.

Gold, Rachel Benson. *Abortion and Women's Health: A Turning Point for America?* New York & Washington, D.C.: Alan Guttmacher Institute, 1990.

Jaffe, F. S., et al. *Abortion Politics: Private Morality and Public Policy.* New York: McGraw-Hill, 1981.

Kushner, Eve. *Experiencing Abortion: A Weaving of Women's Words.* Binghamton, N.Y.: Haworth Press, 1997.

LaFleur, William R. *Liquid Life: Abortion and Buddhism in Japan.* Princeton, N.J.: Princeton University Press, 1992.

Nathanson, Sue, Ph.D. *Soul Crisis: One Woman's Journey through Abortion to Renewal.* New York: Signet, 1990.

Osofsky, J. D., and R. Rajan. *The Abortion Experience: Psychological and Medical Impact.* New York: Harper & Row, 1973.

Riven, Roy. "A Decision between a Woman and God." *Los Angeles Times,* May 24, 1996, sec. E, pp. 1,8.

Sachdev, Paul, ed. *International Handbook on Abortion*. New York, Westport, Conn., and London: Greenwood Press, 1988.

Shostak, Arthur B., and Gary McLouth, with Lynn Seng. *Men and Abortion: Lessons, Losses and Love*. New York: Praeger, 1984.

Townsend, Rita, and Ann Perkins. *Bitter Fruit: Women's Experiences of Unplanned Pregnancy, Abortion, and Adoption*. Alameda, Calif.: Hunter House, 1991.

GENETIC ABORTION

Adler, B., and T. Kushnick. "Genetic Counseling in Prenatally Diagnosed Trisomy 18 and 21: Psychological Aspects." *Pediatrics* 69 (1982): 94–99.

Apodoca, Patrice. "The Politics of Heartbreak: Three Women Concerned about Their Own Health and about Fatal Birth Defects Make the Painful Decision to End Late-Term Pregnancies." *Los Angeles Times/Orange County*, May 7, 1996, sec. E, pp. 4–6.

Donnal, P., N. Charles, and P. Harris. "Attitudes of Patients after 'Genetic' Termination of Pregnancy." *British Medical Journal* 282 (February 21, 1981): 621–22.

Menary, Jean, Ph.D. "The Amniocentesis-Abortion Experience: A Study of the Psychological Effects and Healing." Doctoral dissertation, Harvard University, 1987.

MULTIFETAL REDUCTION

McKinney, Mary, Ph.D., Jennifer Downey, M.D., and Ilan Timor-Tritsch, M.D. "The Psychological Effects of Multifetal Pregnancy Reduction." *Fertility and Sterility* 64, no.1 (July 1995): 68–75.

Walter, Virginia N. "Women's Psychological Responses to

Multifetal Reduction: Implications for Counseling." Presented at Course XI Legal and Bioethical Challenges to Effective Fertility Counseling, sponsored by the American Fertility Society, November 5–6, 1994, pp. 71–78.

PARENTING

Anthony, E., James Benedek, and Therese Benedek, eds. *Parenthood: Its Psychology and Psychopathology.* Boston: Little Brown & Co., 1970.

Benedek, Therese, M.D. "Parenthood as a Developmental Phase: A Contribution to the Libido Theory." *Journal of the American Psychoanalytic Association* 7 (1959): 389–417.

Chodorow, Nancy. *The Reproduction of Mothering: Psychoanalysis and the Sociology of Gender.* Berkeley, Calif.: University of California Press, 1978.

Coleman, Arthur D., and Libby Lee Coleman. *The Father: Mythology and Changing Roles.* Willmette, Ill.: Chiron Publications, 1988.

Deutsch, Helene, M.D. *The Psychology of Women,* vol. 2: *Motherhood.* New York: Grune & Stratton, 1945.

Finzi, Sylvia Vegetti. *Mothering: Toward a New Psychoanalytic Construction.* New York: Guilford Press, 1996.

Gurwitt, Alan R., M.D. "Aspects of Prospective Fatherhood: A Case Report." *Psychoanalytic Study of the Child* 31 (1976): 237–71.

Harding, Esther M. *The Way of All Women.* New York, San Francisco, and London: Harper Colophon Books, 1970.

————. *Woman's Mysteries: Ancient and Modern: A Psychological Interpretation of the Feminine Principle as Portrayed in Myth, Story and Dreams.* New York: Harper & Row, 1976.

Ireland, Mardy S. *Reconceiving Women: Separating Motherhood from Female Identity.* New York and London: Guilford Press, 1993.

Jacobson, Edith, M.D. "Development of the Wish for a Child in Boys." *Psychoanalytic Study of the Child* 5: 139–52.

Rich, Adrienne. *Of Woman Born: Motherhood as Experience and Institution.* New York: W. W. Norton & Co., 1976.

PREGNANCY

Bibring, G., T. Dwyer, D. Huntington, and A. Balenstein. "A Study of the Psychological Processes in Pregnancy and of the Earliest Mother-Child Relationship." *Psychoanalytic Study of the Child* 16 (1961): 9–24.

Chester, Laura, ed. *Cradle and All: Women Writers on Pregnancy and Birth.* Boston and London: Faber & Faber, 1989.

Coleman, Libby Lee, and Arthur D. Coleman. *Pregnancy: The Psychological Experience.* New York: The Noonday Press, 1991.

Jarvis, Wilbur. "Some Effects of Pregnancy and Childbirth on Men." *Journal of the American Psychoanalytic Association* 10 (1962): 689–99.

Liebenberg, Beatrice. "Expectant Fathers." *American Journal of Orthopsychiatry* 37 (1967): 358–59.

Raphael-Leff, J. "Facilitators and Regulators: Conscious and

Unconscious Processes in Pregnancy and Early Motherhood."
British Journal of Medical Psychology 59 (1986): 43–55.

———. *Psychological Processes in Childbearing.* London: Chapman
& Hall, 1991.

INFERTILITY

Fleming, Anne Taylor. "A Fragile Hope." *Parenting* (June/July
1994): 95–97.

———. *Motherhood Deferred: A Woman's Journey.* New York: G. P.
Putnam's Sons, 1994.

Harkness, Carla. *The Infertility Book: A Comprehensive Medical and
Emotional Guide.* Berkeley, Calif.: Celestial Arts, 1992.

May, Elain Tyler. *Barren in the Promised Land: Childless Americans
and the Pursuit of Happiness.* New York: HarperCollins, 1995.

Menning, Barbara Eck. *Infertility: A Guide for the Childless Couple.*
Englewood Cliffs, N.J.: Prentice Hall, 1977.

Salzer, Linda P. *Surviving Infertility: A Compassionate Guide through
the Emotional Crisis of Infertility.* New York: HarperPerennial,
1991.

Shacochis, Bob. "Missing Children: One Couple's Anguished
Attempt to Conceive." *Harper's* (October 1996): 55–63.

MISCELLANEOUS

Engel, Lewis, and Tom Ferguson. *Imaginary Crimes: Why We
Punish Ourselves and How to Stop.* Boston: Houghton-Mifflin Co.,
1990.

Frank, Arthur. *At the Will of the Body*. Boston: Houghton Mifflin Co., 1991.

Winnicott, D. W. *Playing and Reality*. London and New York: Routledge, 1982.

If you have comments and/or experiences you would like to share, please write to:

Unspeakable Losses
1760 Solano Avenue, Suite 300
Berkeley, CA 94707

or e-mail to:

klugerbell@earthlink.net